P9-DEZ-929

A *Taste of the*
COUNTRY

Editor: Jean Van Dyke
Food Editor: Grace Howaniec
Art Director: Jim Sibilski
Art Associates: Peggy Bjorkman, Cindy Weber
Production: Sally Manich, Ellen Baltes
Food Photography: Mike Huibregtse

International Standard Book Number: 0-89821-089-5
Library of Congress Catalog Card Number: 89-61837
© 1989, Reiman Associates Inc.
5400 S. 60th St., Greendale WI 53129
All rights reserved.
Printed in U.S.A.

TO ORDER additional copies of *A Taste of the Country,* Second Edition, send $11.98 each plus $3.00 postage and handling to: Country Store, Code **#5301**, Box 572, Milwaukee WI 53201. To order *A Taste of the Country,* First Edition, send $9.98 each plus $3.00 postage and handling. Use Code **#3018**.

Dishes on cover are pictured on Pg. 22.

Recipes marked with a ✓ use less salt, sugar and fat, and also include *Diabetic Exchanges.*

Chase away winter's chills with these warming homemade dishes—and perhaps cook up a surprise at the same time!

Meat pies were hearty favorites in grandma's generation. They still satisfy country appetites today, and some have gone modern—in taste *and* technique.

Traditional cooks will enjoy practicing their pastry skills on two country classics shown here—Salmon Pie and Chicken Pot Pie with Celery Seed Crust. Busy cooks will

appreciate other picture-perfect pies that offer time-saving crust alternatives such as stuffing mix, refrigerated rolls and potato flakes.

Meat and potato lovers will find their standbys stand out in Swiss Potato Pie and in Meat and Potato Pie...and younger taste buds will be tempted by tantalizing Tostada Grande, tasty Cheeseburger Pie and Pop-up Pizza Pie.

No matter which pie you pick prepare these kitchen- and taste-tested treats with confidence!

MOUTH-WATERING! Clockwise from lower left—**Pop-up Pizza Pie**, Catherine Beach, Redfield, Iowa (Pg. 11); **Salmon Pie**, Edna Hoffman, Hebron, Indiana (Pg. 11); **Tostada Grande**, Jenny Nichols, Conroe, Texas (Pg. 12); **Meat and Potato Pie**, Darlis Anderson, Badger, Iowa (Pg. 11); **Spaghetti Pie**, Ellen Vandyne, Sistersville, West Virginia (Pg. 12); **Chicken Pot Pie with Celery Seed Crust**, Ruth Landis, Manheim, Pennsylvania (Pg. 12); **Cheeseburger Pie**, Margery Bryan, Royal City, Washington (Pg. 12); **Swiss Potato Pie**, Linda Erdy, West Mansfield, Ohio (Pg. 11).

♥ Tasty and traditional meat pies are a meal in themselves, brimming with the unmistakable country goodness of abundant meats, wholesome vegetables and tasty gravy.

MARVELOUS MAINSTAYS. Top to bottom—**Quick Crescent Taco Pie**, Jean Moeller, Pipestone, Minnesota (Pg. 12); **Turkey Turnovers**, Avonel Waller, Lakeland, Florida (Pg. 13); **Tater Crust Tuna Pie**, Cynthia Kolberg, Syracuse, Indiana (Pg. 13); **Chicken and Stuffing Pie**, Ina Schmillen, Elkhorn, Nebraska (Pg. 13).

meals in MINUTES

Recipes from Marjo Green, New Berlin, Wisconsin.

PERFECTING your cooking skills often means learning how to spend *less* time in the kitchen! But it's important not to give up attractive, appetizing meals for the sake of speed, no matter how hectic your day.

It's hard to believe that a satisfying meal such as this one can be ready to eat in less than 30 minutes—but it's true. Once you try it for yourself, you—like other busy cooks who've tried this menu—will add it to your regular meal plans.

And by the way, don't forget to vary the dessert flavor by using different flavors of pudding!

BROILED PORK CHOPS WITH APPLE SLICES

> 4 butterfly OR center-cut loin
>   pork chops, 1 inch thick
> Salt and pepper as desired
> Ground sage
>   1 red cooking apple, cored,
>   sliced in 1/4-inch-thick
>   rounds
> Cinnamon and sugar

Season chops lightly with salt, pepper and sage; place on broiler rack 4 in. from preheated broiler element. Broil 6 minutes; turn. Broil 6 minutes more. Four minutes before chops are done, sprinkle apple slices with cinnamon and sugar and place on broiler rack. When broiling is completed, place an apple slice on top of each pork chop. Serve immediately. **Yield:** 4 servings.

CHOCOLATE ANGEL PARFAIT

> 1 package (6 ounces) *instant*
>   chocolate pudding mix
> 3 cups milk
> Half of an 8-3/4-ounce angel food
>   cake or pound cake
> Whipped topping
> Chocolate chips, shaved chocolate
>   curls or chocolate syrup for
>   garnish

Prepare pudding mix with milk as package directs. Allow pudding to set. Tear cake into bite-sized pieces; place a third of pieces into parfait glasses. Layer half of pudding over cake. Arrange remaining cake into glasses; cover with remaining pudding. Garnish with whipped topping and chocolate garnish. **Yield:** 4 servings.

FLAVORFUL BROCCOLI SAUTE

> 1-1/4 pounds fresh broccoli,
>   washed, drained, separated
>   into flowerets
>   1 to 2 tablespoons butter
>   1 tablespoon lemon juice
>   1 teaspoon sesame oil (optional)
> Salt and pepper to taste

In skillet, saute flowerets in butter for 5 minutes, stirring 2 to 3 times. Add lemon juice, sesame oil, salt and pepper, and serve. **Yield:** 4 servings.

SEEDED BOWTIE NOODLES

> 8 ounces bowtie noodles
> 3 tablespoons butter
> 1 teaspoon poppyseeds
> 1/2 teaspoon salt
> 1/4 teaspoon coarsely ground
>   black pepper

Cook noodles according to package directions, about 15 minutes. Drain; toss gently with remaining ingredients. **Yield:** 4 servings.

> *TABLE TIP: For an attractive, natural table centerpiece for fall, arrange Golden Delicious or Honey Gold apples in a bowl with bright-colored leaves.*

Thank goodness for chocolate! You can always count on chocolate to come through when you need it...rich and soothing, it's one of life's little rewards. You have a variety of "rewards" to choose from here—whether favorite "down-home" recipes or "party-perfect" sweet sensations.

Celebrate Valentine's Day—or any day—by sampling these delectable delights. From cookie jar favorites to traditional candies to the old-fashioned goodness of hot fudge sauce or cake, you'll savor the taste of each and every one.

And, for very special occasions, try one of our "V.I.P.s" (Very Impressive Pies!).

CAPTIVATING CHOCOLATE: Clockwise from lower left—**Hot Fudge Pudding Cake**, Martha Fehl, Brookville, Indiana (Pg. 14); **Double Chocolate Crumble Bars**, Germaine Stank, Pound, Wisconsin (Pg. 14); **Hot Fudge Sauce**, Florence Herman, Fairbury, Nebraska (Pg. 14); **Peanut Chocolate Chip Cookies**, Jodie McCoy, Tulsa, Oklahoma (Pg. 15); **Chocolate Mousse Pie**, Sheryl Goodnough, Eliot, Maine (Pg. 15); **Buckeye Candy**, Bev Spain, Bellville, Ohio (Pg. 14); **German Chocolate Pie**, Crystal Allen, Homer, Illinois (Pg. 15); **Chocolate Ice Cream Pie**, Bill Hughes, Dolores, Colorado (Pg. 14).

Chili, above all other recipes, is a matter of individual taste. Proponents of each kind or style are outspoken in their preferences in seasoning, ingredients and serving style.

Our featured recipes might not change your mind concerning "beans or no beans", but they might tempt "seasoned" cooks into trying someone else's version of chili.

Whatever chili you cook up next—whether it's a time-tested favorite or a taste treat new to you—try it with Gloria Jarrett's butter-rich corn bread!

CHILI CHAMPS. Clockwise from lower left—**Gourmet Chili**, Don Easley, Defiance, Ohio (Pg. 15); **All-American Corn Bread**, Gloria Jarrett, Loveland, Ohio (Pg. 15); **Texas Chili**, Sylvia Dorr, Stratham, New Hampshire (Pg. 16); **Vegetarian Chili**, Jutta Doering, Kelowna, British Columbia (Pg. 16).

SALMON PIE

Edna Hoffman, Hebron, Indiana

(PICTURED ON PAGE 4)

    3 medium potatoes (1 pound),
      peeled and cut into 1/2-inch
      chunks
    2 medium carrots, sliced
    1 medium onion, chopped
    4 tablespoons butter
1/4 cup flour
    1 teaspoon salt
1/4 teaspoon pepper
1/4 teaspoon dill weed
    2 cups milk
    1 can (15-1/2 ounces) salmon,
      drained, skin removed and
      separated into bite-sized
      chunks
    1 cup fresh OR frozen peas
    1 single crust pastry

In saucepan over medium heat, cook potatoes, carrots and onion in butter until almost tender, stirring often. Stir in flour, salt, pepper and dill until blended; cook 1 minute. Gradually stir in milk; cook until the mixture is thickened and smooth, stirring constantly. Gently stir in salmon and peas. Spoon mixture into 2-qt. round casserole; set aside. Roll out your favorite pastry, 1-1/2 in. larger than casserole top. Place pastry loosely over salmon mixture. Trim pastry edge; fold overhang under and crimp edges. Cut slits in pastry top or cut out designs to decorate top of pie. Sprinkle crust with more dill weed, if desired. Bake at 375° for 35-40 minutes or until top is golden brown. **Yield:** 6 servings.

SWISS POTATO PIE

Linda Erdy, West Mansfield, Ohio

(PICTURED ON PAGE 4)

    6 medium-sized potatoes
    6 tablespoons butter, melted
    1 teaspoon salt
1/4 teaspoon pepper
1/4 teaspoon ground nutmeg
    1 teaspoon chopped parsley
1-1/2 cups (6 ounces) diced Swiss
      cheese
    1 cup cubed, cooked ham
    1 medium onion, grated
    3 eggs
1/2 cup milk
Paprika

Peel potatoes and cook in saucepan with water until tender; drain. Mash; stir in butter, salt, pepper, nutmeg and parsley. Spoon about two-thirds of potato mixture on sides and bottom of greased 1-1/2-qt. to 2-qt. baking dish. Set aside. In medium bowl, combine cheese, ham and onion; spoon this mixture into the potato-lined dish. Beat together eggs and milk; pour over ham/cheese. Spoon (or pipe with a pastry tube) remaining potato mixture over top. Sprinkle with paprika. Bake at 400° for 30-35 minutes or until puffed and golden brown. Let stand 10 minutes; cut into serving portions. **Yield:** 4-6 servings.

MEAT AND POTATO PIE

Darlis Anderson, Badger, Iowa

(PICTURED ON PAGE 4)

    3 tablespoons vegetable oil
    3 cups shredded frozen hash
      browns
    1 cup grated Swiss OR cheddar
      cheese
3/4 cup diced ham, sausage or
      chopped chicken
1/4 cup chopped onion
    1 cup evaporated OR whole milk
    2 eggs
1/2 teaspoon salt
1/8 teaspoon pepper
Chopped parsley

Mix together vegetable oil and potatoes in 9-in. pie plate. Press into pie crust shape. Bake at 425° for 15 minutes or until crust begins to brown. Remove from oven. Layer on cheese, meat and onion; set aside. Combine milk, eggs and seasoning in bowl; beat all until blended. Pour egg mixture over layered ingredients. Sprinkle with parsley. Return to oven (same temperature); bake for 30 minutes or until lightly browned. Allow to cool 5 minutes before cutting into wedges. **Yield:** 4-6 servings.

POP-UP PIZZA PIE

Catherine Beach, Redfield, Iowa

(PICTURED ON PAGE 4)

FILLING:
1-1/2 pounds *lean* ground beef
    1 cup chopped onion
    1 cup chopped green pepper
    1 clove garlic, minced
1/2 teaspoon oregano
1/2 cup water
1/8 teaspoon Tabasco sauce
    1 can (15-ounces) tomato sauce
    1 envelope (1.5 ounces)
      spaghetti sauce mix
POPOVER BATTER:
    1 cup milk
    1 tablespoon vegetable oil
    2 eggs
    1 cup flour
1/2 teaspoon salt

    6 to 8 ounces sliced mozzarella
      OR Monterey Jack cheese
1/2 cup grated Parmesan cheese

In large skillet, brown the ground beef. Drain well. Stir in onion, green pepper, garlic, oregano, water, Tabasco sauce, tomato sauce and spaghetti sauce mix; simmer 10 minutes, stirring occasionally. Set aside. In small bowl, combine milk, oil and eggs; beat 1 minute at medium speed. Lightly stir and spoon flour into measuring cup; level off. Add flour and salt; beat 2 minutes at medium speed of mixer or until smooth. Pour hot meat mixture into ungreased 13-in. x 9-in. pan (or pan of choice). Top with sliced cheese. Pour batter over cheese, covering filling completely; sprinkle with Parmesan cheese. Bake at 400° for 25 to 30 minutes or until puffed and deep golden brown. Serve immediately. **Yield:** 10 servings.

MEAT PIE TIP: Substitute onion salt for regular salt to add flavor to your meat pie pastry.

TURKEY/CHEESE PIE

Ann Davis, Dillsburg, Pennsylvania

    1 pound ground turkey
1-1/2 cups chopped onion
1-1/2 cups milk
3/4 cup baking mix
    3 eggs
1/2 teaspoon seasoned salt
1/4 teaspoon pepper
    2 tomatoes, sliced
    1 cup shredded cheddar cheese

Cook and stir turkey and onion in skillet over medium heat until turkey is browned; drain. Spread in a greased 10-in. pie plate; set aside. Beat milk, baking mix, eggs, salt and pepper in blender or with hand mixer till smooth. Pour into turkey-lined pie plate. Bake 25 minutes at 400°. Top with tomatoes; sprinkle with cheese. Bake until knife inserted in center comes out clean, about 5-8 minutes more. Cool 5 minutes. **Yield:** 6-8 servings.

TOSTADA GRANDE

Jenny Nichols, Conroe, Texas

(PICTURED ON PAGE 5)

1 pound *lean* ground beef
2 tablespoons (1/2 package) taco OR chili seasoning mix
1 can (8 ounces) tomato sauce
1 can (4 ounces) diced green chilies, *drained*
3 to 4 drops Tabasco sauce
1 can (8 ounces) crescent dinner rolls OR 1 can (7.5 ounces) refrigerated biscuits
1 cup refried beans
4 ounces shredded cheese (cheddar and mozzarella mixture preferred)
1/2 head lettuce, shredded
1 large tomato, chopped
1 small onion, chopped

In large skillet, brown ground beef; drain well. Stir in seasoning, tomato sauce, chilies and Tabasco sauce; heat until hot and bubbly. Simmer, uncovered, for 15 minutes or until mixture thickens. Lightly grease 9-in. or 10-in. pie plate. Separate rolls or biscuits; arrange in pans. Press over bottom and up sides to form crust. Spread beans over dough; top with meat mixture. Bake at 375° for 18 to 22 minutes or until crust is golden brown. Sprinkle immediately with cheese. Garnish with lettuce, tomato and onion. **Yield: 4-6 servings.**

CHEESEBURGER PIE

Margery Bryan, Royal City, Washington

(PICTURED ON PAGE 5)

DOUGH:
1 cup packaged baking mix
1/4 cup cold water

FILLING:
1/2 cup chopped onion
1/2 cup chopped green pepper
2 tablespoons butter
1/2 cup lean ground beef
1/2 teaspoon salt
1/4 teaspoon pepper
2 tablespoons packaged baking mix
1 tablespoon Worcestershire sauce
2 eggs
1 cup small curd creamed cottage cheese (drain excess liquid)

TOPPING:
2 medium tomatoes, sliced paper thin

1 cup shredded cheddar cheese, about 4 ounces

In bowl, mix 1 cup baking mix with water until soft dough forms; beat vigorously 20 strokes. Gently smooth dough into a ball on a floured, cloth-covered board. Knead five times. Roll dough 2 in. larger than inverted 9-in. deep dish pie plate. Ease into plate; flute edge if desired. Saute chopped onion and green pepper in butter until tender. Do not brown. Remove onion and green pepper; set aside. Brown ground beef; drain. Remove from heat; stir in reserved onion and green pepper, salt, pepper, 2 tablespoons baking mix and Worcestershire sauce. Spoon into pie crust; set aside. Mix eggs and cottage cheese in bowl; pour over beef mixture. Arrange tomato slices in circle on top; sprinkle with cheese. Bake at 375° about 30 minutes, until set. **Yield: 6-8 servings.**

SPAGHETTI PIE

Ellen Vandyne, Sistersville, West Virginia

(PICTURED ON PAGE 5)

1 package (7 ounces) spaghetti
2 tablespoons butter
1/3 cup Parmesan cheese
2 eggs, well-beaten
1 cup cottage cheese
1 pound *lean* ground beef
1/2 cup chopped onion
1/4 cup chopped green pepper
1 jar (15-1/2 ounces) spaghetti sauce
1/2 cup shredded mozzarella cheese

Cook spaghetti according to package directions; drain. Add butter, cheese and eggs to hot spaghetti. Form mixture into "crust" in 10-in. pie plate. Microwave (MW) on HIGH 2 minutes. Spread cottage cheese over spaghetti crust. Set aside. MW on HIGH crumbled ground beef in microwaveable colander for 5 minutes; drain all fat. Add onion and green pepper to ground beef in bowl; MW on HIGH for 2-3 minutes. Stir in spaghetti sauce; MW, covered, on HIGH for 5-7 minutes. Stir; add this mixture to spaghetti crust covered with cheese. MW 6-8 minutes, turning once. Sprinkle mozzarella cheese on top. MW on HIGH for 1 minute or until cheese melts. CONVENTIONAL METHOD: Follow procedure above, using skillet to cook meat on stove, but do not pre-bake spaghetti "crust". Layer in-

gredients according to instructions. Bake, uncovered, at 350° for 20 minutes. Sprinkle cheese on top; return to oven for 5 minutes. **Yield: 6 servings.**

CHICKEN POT PIE WITH CELERY SEED CRUST

Ruth Landis, Manheim, Pennsylvania

(PICTURED ON PAGE 5)

FILLING:
1/3 cup butter
1/3 cup flour
1/3 cup chopped onion
1/2 teaspoon salt
1/4 teaspoon pepper
1-3/4 cups chicken broth
2/3 cup milk
2 cups cut-up cooked chicken
1 package (10-ounces) frozen peas and carrots

PASTRY:
2 cups flour
2 teaspoons celery seed
1 teaspoon salt
2/3 cup plus 2 tablespoons shortening
4 to 5 tablespoons ice water

In saucepan, melt butter over low heat. Blend in flour, onion and seasonings. Cook, stirring, until mixture is bubbly. Remove from heat and stir in chicken broth and milk. Heat to boiling, stirring constantly. Boil; stir 1 minute. Gently stir in chicken and frozen vegetables; set aside. Prepare pastry by measuring flour, celery seed and salt in bowl. Cut in shortening. Sprinkle in water 1 tablespoon at a time, mixing until all flour is moistened and dough almost cleans sides of bowl. Gather dough into ball. On lightly floured board, roll two-thirds of the dough into a 13-in. square. Ease pastry into 9-in. x 9-in. square pan. Pour filling into pan. Roll remaining dough into square; place over filling. Cut slits in center to allow steam to escape. Bake at 425° for 30-35 minutes. **Yield: 4-6 servings.**

QUICK CRESCENT TACO PIE

Jean Moeller, Pipestone, Minnesota

(PICTURED ON PAGE 6)

1-1/4 pounds lean ground beef
1 package taco seasoning mix
1/2 cup water
1/2 cup chunky salsa
1 can (8 ounces) crescent dinner rolls

1-1/2 cups crushed corn chips
1 carton (8 ounces) dairy sour
   cream
6 slices American cheese
Shredded lettuce
Sliced black olives
Diced tomatoes

Brown meat in large skillet; drain. Add seasoning mix, water and salsa; simmer for 5 minutes. Spread the crescent roll dough in 10-in. pie plate to form crust; press edges together at seams. Sprinkle 1 cup corn chips on crust bottom, reserving remaining 1/2 cup. Spoon on meat mixture. Spread sour cream over meat. Cover with cheese slices; sprinkle on remaining 1/2 cup of corn chips. Bake at 375° for 20 minutes, until crust is golden brown. Serve with lettuce, olives and tomatoes. **Yield:** 6 servings.

TATER CRUST TUNA PIE

Cynthia Kolberg, Syracuse, Indiana

(PICTURED ON PAGE 6)

CRUST:
1 cup flour
1/2 cup mashed potato flakes
1/2 cup butter
3 to 4 tablespoons ice water
1 can (2.8 ounces) french-fried
   onions, *divided*

FILLING:
3/4 cup mashed potato flakes
1 cup shredded cheddar
   cheese, *divided*
2 tablespoons chopped stuffed
   green olives
1 can (6-1/2 ounces) tuna,
   drained
1 can (10-3/4 ounces)
   condensed cream of
   mushroom soup, reduced
   sodium preferred
1 egg

In medium bowl, combine the flour and potato flakes; cut in butter until crumbly. Add water, 1 tablespoon at a time, until dough is just moist enough to hold together. Press pastry over bottom and up sides of ungreased 9-in. or 10-in. pie plate. Flute edge. Reserve 1/2 cup onions; set aside. Sprinkle remaining onions into pastry shell. In medium bowl, combine all filling ingredients except 1/2 cup of cheese. Spoon tuna filling into pastry crust. Bake at 350° for 25-30 minutes or until crust is golden. Sprin-

kle with reserved cheese and onions; bake for an additional 5-10 minutes or until cheese is melted. Let stand 5 minutes before serving. **Yield:** 6-8 servings.

CHICKEN AND STUFFING PIE

Ina Schmillen, Elkhorn, Nebraska

(PICTURED ON PAGE 6)

CRUST:
1 package (8 ounces) herb
   seasoning stuffing mix
3/4 cup chicken broth
1/2 cup butter, melted
1 egg, beaten

FILLING:
1 can (4 ounces) mushrooms,
   drained, *reserve liquid*
2 tablespoons flour
1/2 cup chopped onion
1 tablespoon butter
1 can (10 ounces) chicken
   gravy mix OR 1 jar (12 ounces)
1 teaspoon Worcestershire sauce
1/2 teaspoon thyme
3 cups cubed, cooked chicken
1 cup fresh OR frozen peas
2 tablespoons diced pimiento
1 tablespoon parsley flakes
4 ounces sliced Colby OR
   American cheese

Mix crust ingredients in medium bowl; press into 10-in. greased pie plate. Set aside. Combine mushroom liquid with flour in small bowl; set aside. In saucepan on top of stove, saute mushrooms and onion in butter. Stir in all remaining ingredients except cheese. Heat thoroughly; turn into stuffing crust. Bake at 375° for 20 minutes. Cut each cheese slice into strips; place in lattice design on pie. Bake 5 minutes more. **Yield:** 6-8 servings.

TURKEY TURNOVERS

Avonel Waller, Lakeland, Florida

(PICTURED ON PAGE 6)

FILLING:
1 cup chopped celery
1/4 cup chopped onion
1/4 cup butter
1/3 cup flour
1 to 2 teaspoons salt
1/4 teaspoon pepper
1-1/4 cups milk
4 cups cooked, cubed turkey
1/4 cup chopped parsley

DOUGH:

4 cups flour
1 teaspoon salt
1-1/2 cups butter
2 cups (8 ounces) shredded
   sharp cheddar cheese
2 cups dairy sour cream

In large skillet on top of stove, cook celery and onion in butter until tender. Blend in flour, salt and pepper. Gradually add milk; cook, stirring constantly, until thickened. Add turkey and parsley. Set aside. In large bowl, combine flour and salt; cut in butter until mixture resembles coarse crumbs. Stir in the cheese. Add sour cream, mixing until dough forms a ball. Divide dough in half. Roll out half of dough into 18-in. x 12-in. rectangle. Cut into six 6-in. squares. Repeat with second half of dough. Place 1/3 cup turkey filling on each square. Fold diagonally to form a triangle; seal edges by pressing down with fork tines. Cut slits in top of turnovers. Place on cookie sheet. Bake at 450° for 10 minutes; reduce heat to 400°. Bake 5-8 minutes more until the crust is golden brown. **Yield:** 12 turnovers.

HAMBURGER UPSIDE DOWN PIE

Dianna Eperthener, Grove City, Pennsylvania

FILLING:
1 pound *lean* ground beef
2 tablespoons vegetable oil
1 cup chopped celery
1/4 cup minced onion
3/4 cup chopped green pepper
1 teaspoon salt
1/4 teaspoon pepper
1/2 clove garlic, minced
1 can (10-1/2 ounces) tomato
   soup

PARSLEY BISCUIT TOPPING:
1/2 cup shortening
2 cups all-purpose flour
3 teaspoons baking powder
1 teaspoon salt
1/4 cup minced parsley
1 cup milk

Brown ground beef in oil in 10-in. ovenproof skillet. Add remaining filling ingredients; simmer 10 minutes. Meanwhile, make biscuits by cutting shortening into sifted dry ingredients in medium bowl. Stir in milk only until flour is moistened. Drop biscuit topping by spoonful over hot mixture in skillet. Bake at 425° for 20 minutes. (You may serve this from the skillet or turn out on platter.) Serve immediately. **Yield:** 6 servings.

DOUBLE CHOCOLATE CRUMBLE BARS
Germaine Stank, Pound, Wisconsin

(PICTURED ON PAGE 8)

BARS:
- 1/2 cup butter
- 3/4 cup sugar
- 2 eggs
- 1 teaspoon vanilla
- 3/4 cup all-purpose flour
- 1/2 cup chopped pecans
- 2 tablespoons unsweetened cocoa
- 1/4 teaspoon baking powder
- 1/4 teaspoon salt

TOPPING:
- 2 cups miniature marshmallows
- 1 package (6 ounces) semisweet chocolate chips
- 1 cup creamy peanut butter
- 1-1/2 cups crisp rice cereal

Cream butter and sugar; beat in eggs and vanilla. Set aside. Stir together flour, chopped nuts, cocoa, baking powder and salt; stir into egg mixture. Spread in bottom of greased 13-in. x 9-in. x 2-in. baking pan. Bake at 350° for 15-20 minutes or until bars test done. Sprinkle marshmallows evenly on top; bake 3 minutes more. Cool. In small saucepan, combine chocolate chips and peanut butter; cook and stir over low heat until chocolate is melted. Stir in cereal. Spread mixture on top of cooled bars. Chill; cut in bars. Refrigerate. **Yield:** 3-4 dozen bars.

CHOCOLATE ICE CREAM PIE
Bill Hughes, Dolores, Colorado

(PICTURED ON PAGE 8)

- 2 8-inch chocolate wafer pie shells
- 2 pints gourmet vanilla ice cream
- 1 box (3 ounces) *instant* chocolate fudge pudding mix
- 1 box (6 ounces) *instant* French vanilla pudding mix
- 2 cups *extra heavy* whipping cream
- 1/2 cup coffee-flavored liqueur
- 4 ounces vanilla yogurt
- 6 ounces (6 squares) unsweetened chocolate, grated

Melt ice cream; set aside. In separate bowl, blend the puddings with whipping cream and liqueur. Mix with electric mixer until stiff. Add mixture to melted ice cream, stirring to blend.

Blend in yogurt and grated chocolate. Pour into pie shells or into springform pans (as shown) and freeze until firm. Garnish with additional whipped cream and chocolate curls, if desired. **Yield:** 2 pies.

TOPPING TIP: To thaw frozen whipped topping (4-1/2-oz. carton) microwave on DEFROST/LOW for 30-60 seconds.

FASTER DEFROSTING: When freezing ground beef for storage, form into doughnut-shaped portions; the meat will defrost more evenly this way. To use, microwave on DEFROST/LOW for 3 minutes; let stand for 5 minutes. Open wrap, turn meat over and microwave for 3 more minutes on DEFROST/LOW.

BUCKEYE CANDY
Bev Spain, Bellville, Ohio

(PICTURED ON PAGE 9)

CANDY:
- 1 stick *softened* butter OR margarine
- 1-3/4 cups (1 18-ounce jar) creamy peanut butter
- 1 teaspoon vanilla
- About 1 pound confectioners' sugar

CHOCOLATE COATING:
- 1 package (12 ounces) semi-sweet chocolate chips
- 1 tablespoon vegetable shortening

Cream butter, peanut butter and vanilla together adding confectioners' sugar until proper consistency is reached. Roll candy into 1-in. balls and place on wax paper-lined cookie sheet. Melt chips and shortening together in top of double boiler. Keep chocolate mixture in double boiler over low heat while you dip each candy. Using a toothpick, dip each ball covering about three-fourths of candy. (Peanut butter needs to show for an authentic buckeye.) Return candy to sheet to cool. **Yield:** 8 dozen buckeyes.

HOT FUDGE PUDDING CAKE
Martha Fehl, Brookville, Indiana

(PICTURED ON PAGE 8)

PUDDING CAKE:
- 1 cup all-purpose flour
- 2 teaspoons baking powder
- 1/4 teaspoon salt
- 1 cup unsweetened cocoa
- 1 cup sugar
- About 1/2 cup milk
- 2 tablespoons shortening, melted
- 1 teaspoon vanilla
- 1 cup broken pecans OR walnuts

SAUCE:
- 1-1/2 cups brown sugar
- 5 tablespoons cocoa
- 1-3/4 cups hot water

Mix together flour, baking powder, salt, cocoa and sugar. Stir in milk, melted shortening and vanilla (mixture will be very stiff). Blend in nuts. Spread mixture in 8- or 9-in. square pan. To make sauce, sprinkle brown sugar and cocoa over batter; pour hot water over all. Bake at 350° for 45 minutes. Serve warm with scoop of vanilla ice cream. **Yield:** 8-10 servings.

HOT FUDGE SAUCE
Florence Herman, Fairbury, Nebraska

(PICTURED ON PAGE 8)

- 3 ounces (3 squares) unsweetened chocolate
- 5 tablespoons butter OR margarine
- 3 cups (14 ounces) sifted confectioners' sugar
- 1/8 teaspoon salt
- 1 cup evaporated milk
- 1 teaspoon vanilla

Melt chocolate and butter/margarine in saucepan over very low heat. Stir in sugar and salt, alternately with milk, blending well with wire whisk. Bring mixture to boil over medium heat, stirring constantly. Stir while cooking until mixture becomes thick and creamy, about 8 minutes. Stir in vanilla. Serve warm over ice cream. **Yield:** About 1-1/2 pints.

(PICTURED ON PAGE 9)

GERMAN CHOCOLATE PIE
Crystal Allen, Homer, Illinois

(PICTURED ON PAGE 9)

1 9-inch *unbaked* pie shell, (deep dish)
1 package (4 ounces) German sweet chocolate
1/4 cup butter
1 can (12 ounces) evaporated milk
1-1/2 cups sugar
3 tablespoons cornstarch
1/8 teaspoon salt
2 eggs
1 teaspoon vanilla
1-1/2 cups coconut
1 cup pecans, chopped

Melt chocolate and butter over low heat. Remove from heat; blend in milk. Set aside. Mix sugar, cornstarch and salt together. Beat in eggs and vanilla. Blend in chocolate mixture; pour into pie shell. Combine coconut and nuts; sprinkle on top of chocolate mixture. Bake at 375° for 45 minutes. **Yield:** 1 pie.

PEANUT CHOCOLATE CHIP COOKIES
Jodie McCoy, Tulsa, Oklahoma

(PICTURED ON PAGE 9)

2 cups flour
2 teaspoons baking powder
1/2 teaspoon salt
1 cup margarine
1 cup granulated sugar
1 cup brown sugar
2 eggs
1 teaspoon vanilla
1 cup creamy peanut butter
1 cup Spanish peanuts
1 cup chocolate chips

Combine dry ingredients; set aside. Cream shortening and sugars; add eggs and vanilla and beat until fluffy. Blend in peanut butter. Gradually add dry ingredients. Stir in peanuts and chocolate chips. Drop by teaspoonfuls or #100 scoop onto greased cookie sheet. Bake at 350° for about 8 minutes. **Yield:** 7-8 dozen.

CHOCOLATE MOUSSE PIE
Sheryl Goodnough, Eliot, Maine

(PICTURED ON PAGE 9)

4 ounces semisweet chocolate
1/3 cup milk, divided
2 tablespoons sugar
1 package (3 ounces) cream cheese, softened
1 carton (8 ounces) nondairy topping
Peppermint flavoring to taste OR flavor of choice
1 8-inch chocolate wafer crust

Heat chocolate and *2 tablespoons milk* in medium saucepan over low heat, stirring until chocolate is melted. Set aside. Beat sugar into cream cheese; add remaining milk and chocolate mixture. Beat until smooth. Fold chocolate mixture into the whipped topping; blend till smooth. Add peppermint flavoring to taste, if desired. Spoon filling into pie crust or springform pan, as shown. Freeze until firm, about 4 hours. Store any leftovers in freezer. **Yield:** 1 pie.

ALL-AMERICAN CORNBREAD
Gloria and Charles Jarrett, Loveland, Ohio

(PICTURED ON PAGE 10)

2 cups biscuit mix
1 cup butter
1 cup half-and-half
1 cup yellow cornmeal
1/2 teaspoon baking soda
1/2 teaspoon salt
3/4 cup sugar
2 eggs, slightly beaten

Scald cream with butter; add to thoroughly mixed dry ingredients. Mix in eggs. Pour into greased and floured 13- x 9- x 2-in. pan. Bake at 350° for 30 minutes. Allow to stand for several minutes before cutting. **Yield:** 12 servings.

GOURMET CHILI
Don Easley, Defiance, Ohio

(PICTURED ON PAGE 10)

1-1/2 cups dry pinto beans*
2 quarts water
1/2 pound ground pure beef suet (necessary for flavor)
1 large sweet onion, chopped fine
2 pounds lean beef, coarse ground OR cut into 1/4-inch cubes
Up to 6 level tablespoons chili powder OR amount to your taste
8 teaspoons cumin powder OR 1-1/2 tablespoons cumin seed
8 teaspoons paprika
1 teaspoon white pepper
1 teaspoon salt OR to taste
6 cloves crushed garlic OR 2 teaspoons garlic powder
Up to 1 level teaspoon cayenne pepper OR to taste
2 tablespoons unsweetened cocoa powder
1 can (4 ounces) green chilies, sliced thin
1 cup tomato juice, *if needed to thin chili*
Sour cream for garnish

*Can substitute 2 cans (15-1/2 ounces *each*) pinto beans, undrained, instead of dry pinto beans, and 2 quarts of water. Soak beans in water to cover overnight; drain. Cover with 2 quarts water; simmer, covered, for 1-1/2 to 2 hours until done. Drain, *reserving 1 cup of cooking water,* set aside. In large 3-quart Dutch oven or heavy kettle, melt suet. Add onion; saute over medium heat until transparent. Add meat and brown, stirring often. Pour off all but 2 tablespoons of fat; add remaining ingredients, except sour cream, *reserved beans* and tomato juice. Cover; simmer for 1-1/2 hours, stirring often and adding up to 1 cup of tomato juice to keep chili to a medium consistency. If a thinner chili is desired, use reserved bean juice. To serve, add warm pinto beans to chili or serve as a side dish. Whichever you prefer. Add a dollop of sour cream in the center of each bowl, taking a bit of sour cream with each spoon of chili. This is a *spicy, meaty* chili. **Yield:** 2 quarts.

CHILI CHARM: *If your young chili eaters don't like beans, try this trick: Mash the beans so they thicken the soup but are invisible to little eyes.*

TEXAS CHILI

Sylvia Dorr, Stratham, New Hampshire

(PICTURED ON PAGE 10)

2-1/2 pounds cubed beef stew meat
Beer (enough to marinate the beef)
1/2 cup shortening
1 cup chopped green peppers
1 cup chopped onions
4 cups chopped fresh tomatoes
1-3/4 cups tomato sauce
5-1/2 cups cooked pinto beans, *drained*
2 tablespoons chili powder
4 teaspoons salt
1-1/2 teaspoons garlic salt
Up to 1/4 cup chopped jalapeno pepper*
1/8 cup vegetable oil
4 teaspoons cumin
1 teaspoon oregano
Up to 5 teaspoons Tabasco sauce*

*This is a *medium hot* chili—reduce jalapeno peppers and Tabasco sauce for a milder chili. Marinate beef in beer for at least 8 hours. Drain beef; pat dry on paper towels. Brown in hot shortening in large kettle. Add peppers, onions, tomatoes, tomato sauce and beans; cook on medium heat for 1 hour. Add spices, Tabasco and jalapeno peppers; cook for 2 more hours. **Yield:** About 4 quarts.

VEGETARIAN CHILI

Jutta Doering, Kelowna, British Columbia

(PICTURED ON PAGE 10)

3 tablespoons vegetable oil, *divided*
1-1/2 to 2 cups onion, chopped
3 cloves garlic, minced
4 ounces fresh mushrooms, sliced
1 large green pepper, chopped
3 stalks celery, sliced
1/2 cup chopped carrot
2 tablespoons chili powder
1-1/2 teaspoons ground cumin
1/2 teaspoon basil, crushed
1/4 teaspoon oregano, ground
1/4 teaspoon marjoram, crushed
1/2 teaspoon black pepper
1 can (15 ounces) tomato sauce
1 can (14 ounces) plum tomatoes in juice
1/3 cup *extra-spicy* catsup
1/4 teaspoon Worcestershire sauce
3/4 cup medium grain bulgur wheat
1 can (6 ounces) vegetable juice
1 can (19 ounces) red kidney
beans, drained
1 can (19 ounces) cannellini beans, drained
1 can (3.25 ounces) pitted ripe olives, drained and sliced

In large kettle, heat 2 tablespoons oil. Add onion and garlic. Cook 5 minutes until onion is tender. Add mushrooms, green peppers, celery, carrot, chili powder, cumin, basil, oregano, marjoram and pepper. Saute 8 minutes or until vegetables are tender. Add tomato sauce, tomatoes and juice, catsup and Worcestershire sauce. Cover and simmer 30 minutes. Meanwhile, heat remaining 1 tablespoon oil in skillet. Add bulgur wheat; cook for 10 minutes. Add vegetable juice; cover and simmer 10-15 minutes. Stir wheat and beans into kettle. Simmer, uncovered, 30 minutes. Stir in olives. **Yield:** 2-1/4 quarts.

BEEF CABBAGE ROLLS

Pat Ehmke, Chanute, Kansas

1 pound *lean* ground chuck
1 small head cabbage, finely chopped
1/8 teaspoon garlic salt
Salt and pepper to taste
1/4 cup water
1 package (8 ounces) crescent dinner rolls
1 cup grated cheddar cheese, optional

In large skillet on top of stove, brown ground chuck; drain excess fat. Add cabbage, garlic salt, salt, pepper and water; stir thoroughly. Cover; cook for about 15 minutes over medium heat. Place crescent rolls, two together, so that they form a rectangle on a lightly greased baking sheet. Spoon meat mixture onto rolls; fold two opposite corners to the center and crimp edges with fork and pierce top. Bake at 350° for 10 minutes or until rolls are brown. Remove from oven; rub tops with butter, if desired. Top with grated cheese; serve immediately. **Yield:** 4 servings.

TASTY TACO PIE

Barbara Cusman, Ashtabula, Ohio

1 *unbaked* pie shell, your own or frozen
1 pound lean ground beef
1 package taco seasoning mix
Water
1 container alfalfa sprouts
1 medium tomato, chopped
1 avocado, sliced
1-1/2 cups cheddar cheese, finely shredded
3/4 cup black (pitted) olives, chopped
1 container (12 ounces) dairy sour cream
Salsa

Bake pie shell according to package directions; cool. Brown ground beef in skillet; drain fat. Add taco seasoning mix and water to meat according to package directions. Simmer 15 minutes. Layer pie in following order: alfalfa sprouts, tomato, avocado, meat mixture, cheese, black olives, dollops of sour cream. Serve with salsa. **Yield:** 4 servings.

CHICKEN CRESCENTS

Kay Smithhisler, Polk, Ohio

2 cups diced, *cooked* chicken
1 package (3 ounces) cream cheese
3/4 cup cream of chicken soup
2 teaspoons milk
1/4 teaspoon salt
1/8 teaspoon pepper
1 package (8 ounces) crescent dinner rolls
2 tablespoons butter, melted
About 2 cups seasoned crushed croutons

In medium bowl, mix chicken, cream cheese, soup, milk and spices. Separate crescent rolls so that you have four squares; press each very flat. Spoon 1/2 cup chicken mixture into half of each square. Fold other half (at perforation) and seal. Brush top and bottom with melted butter and roll each crescent in crushed croutons. Place on cookie sheet. Bake at 350° for 25 minutes. **Yield:** 4 chicken crescents.

MEXICAN BEEF SALAD

Janet Cantrell, Tulsa, Oklahoma

DRESSING:
- 1 cup mayonnaise
- 1 can (4-ounce) chopped green chilies, drained
- 2 tablespoons milk
- 1 teaspoon chili powder
- 1/4 teaspoon salt

SALAD:
- 1 small head iceberg lettuce, shredded
- 1/2 pound roast beef, cut in 1/2-inch-thick strips
- 4 ounces Monterey Jack cheese, cubed
- 2 medium tomatoes, diced
- 1 avocado, peeled, chopped
- 1/2 cup pitted ripe olives

Tortilla chips

Combine mayonnaise, chilies, milk, chili powder and salt; mix well. Chill. Arrange lettuce, meat, cheese, tomatoes, avocado and olives on large serving platter. Spoon mayonnaise mixture into center; surround with tortilla chips. Serve immediately with extra mayonnaise mixture and chips. **Yield: 6-8 servings.**

GRILLED SIRLOIN WITH SAUCE

Lucille Jaeger, Manitowoc, Wisconsin

MARINADE/SAUCE:
- 2 cloves garlic, minced
- 2 tablespoons olive oil OR vegetable oil
- 1/2 cup red wine vinegar
- 1/3 cup catsup
- 1 tablespoon Worcestershire sauce
- 1 teaspoon sugar OR to taste
- 1 teaspoon dried basil, crushed
- 3 pounds lean sirloin steak, cut 1-1/2 inches thick
- 1 can (4-ounce) sliced mushrooms, drained
- 1/4 cup green onions, bias-cut 1/4 inch
- 1/4 cup sliced, pitted ripe olives

In small saucepan, cook garlic in oil until tender. Remove from heat. Stir in vinegar, catsup, Worcestershire sauce, sugar and basil. Set aside. Slash fat on steak edges at 1-in. intervals. Place meat in heavy zip-lock plastic bag; pour in marinade. Seal; refrigerate 6 hours or overnight, turning several times. Drain meat, *reserving marinade.* Pat meat with paper toweling. Place on grill with medium coals for 10-15 minutes, brushing occasionally with marinade. Turn; grill other side 10-15 minutes for *medium-well* doneness. Brush with marinade throughout grilling. Meanwhile, combine reserved marinade, mushrooms, onions and olives in small saucepan. Heat. Remove meat to platter; spoon sauce over meat. **Yield: 8 servings.**

ROAST BEEF, MUSHROOM AND TOMATO SALAD

Dolores Bergs, Marathon, Wisconsin

- 12 ounces cooked roast beef, cut in thin strips
- 8 ounces fresh mushrooms, sliced (about 2-1/2 cups)

FRENCH DRESSING:
- 1/2 cup lemon juice
- 2 cloves garlic, crushed
- 1 tablespoon prepared white horseradish
- 1 teaspoon dry mustard
- 1 teaspoon salt
- 1/4 teaspoon ground pepper
- 1 cup oil, olive OR vegetable
- 3 cups cherry tomatoes
- 2 tablespoons chopped fresh parsley

Put beef and mushrooms in large shallow bowl; add just enough dressing to coat. Let stand 1 hour at room temperature OR refrigerate 24 hours. Add tomatoes; toss. Mound salad on serving platter; sprinkle with parsley. Pass dressing. **Yield: 6 servings.**

COMPANY BEEF CASSEROLE

Carolina Hofeldt, Lloyd, Montana

- 1-1/2 pounds ground beef
- 1/2 cup chopped onions
- 1 tablespoon butter
- 1 can (16 ounces) tomato sauce
- 1 teaspoon sugar
- 1 package (8 ounces) noodles
- 1 cup cottage cheese
- 1 package (8 ounces) cream cheese
- 1/4 cup cultured sour cream
- 1/4 cup chopped green onions
- 1/4 cup chopped green pepper
- 1 teaspoon salt
- 1/4 teaspoon pepper
- 1/8 teaspoon garlic powder
- 2 tablespoons melted butter
- 1/2 cup Parmesan cheese

Brown ground beef and onions in butter; drain fat. Stir in tomato sauce and sugar; set aside. Boil noodles according to package instructions; drain. Combine cheeses, sour cream, green onions, green pepper, salt, pepper and garlic powder; set aside. Butter 3-qt. casserole dish; pour in half the meat mixture; layer with half of noodles. Cover with all of cheese mixture. Top with remaining noodles. Pour melted butter over casserole; top with remaining meat sauce. Sprinkle with Parmesan cheese. Bake at 350° for 30 minutes. **Yield: 10 servings. Diabetic Exchanges:** One serving equals 3 protein, 1 bread, 2 vegetable, 3 fats; also, 463 calories, 717 mg sodium, 126 mg cholesterol, 23 gm carbohydrate.

CHEESE SHARPENER: When a recipe calls for sharp cheddar cheese and you haven't any on hand, a dash of pepper, dry mustard and Worcestershire sauce added to mild cheese will give it a sharp flavor.
SEASONED SALT: Fill a shaker with a mixture of salt, pepper, onion powder, garlic powder and other favorite, often used seasonings. Then when seasoning meat and vegetables, you'll only need to take one shaker from the shelf.

✓ VIRGO-STYLE LAMB

Michelle Hemmer, Mansfield, Washington

MARINADE:
- 1 cup lemon juice
- 1 tablespoon oregano
- 1 tablespoon parsley flakes
- 1 teaspoon garlic powder
- 1/2 teaspoon onion powder
- 1 teaspoon black pepper
- 1 teaspoon seasoning salt
- 4 to 6 lamb chops or steaks OR cubes (1-1/2 inch)

Mix marinade ingredients together in mixing bowl. Place lamb in heavy zip-lock plastic bag; pour marinade over all. Seal; refrigerate for 6-12 hours, turning bag over once. Drain lamb; place on greased grill. Grill 4-5 minutes per side; turning several times. Brush with marinade. **Yield: 4 servings. Diabetic Exchanges:** One serving equals 3 protein, 1/2 fruit, 2 fats; also, 355 calories, 607 mg sodium, 95 mg cholesterol, 5 gm carbohydrates.

Country Inns

Wakulla Springs Lodge
Wakulla Springs, Florida 32305
904/224-5950

Directions: From Tallahassee, take State Road 61 south (15 miles from downtown) to 267; east to Wakulla Springs State Park entrance.

Owner: State of Florida. The lodge and conference center are administered by Florida State Univ., the park by the Department of Natural Resources. (Park office number: 904/222-7279.)
General Manager: John Puskar
Sales Director: John Harvey

Schedule: Open year-round. Dining room serves breakfast, lunch and dinner; meals extra.

Rates and Accommodations: 27 rooms with private baths, air-conditioned, $40-$70 single, $47-$70 double. Conference rooms available. Visa, Master Card. Hours and rates are subject to change. Please call or write.

The "Old Florida" feeling of Wakulla Springs extends to the menu at this low-key lodge.

Pan-fried chicken, flaky biscuits, grits, oysters and fresh local seafood are among the specialties graciously served in Wakulla's big-windowed dining room.

For instance, sample a combination of fresh seafood, such as lightly breaded sea scallops, breaded red snapper fingers, broiled gulf shrimp and a crab cake, accompanied by a crisp green salad, with homemade dressing, a choice of potato and warm homemade rolls. Finish it off with a tart slice of Key Lime pie!

Guests return to Wakulla time and again, to enjoy its 4,000-acre wildlife sanctuary, spring-bank location, relaxing ambience and favorite dishes such as these:

BLUEBERRY SOUR CREAM PIE

- 1 cup sugar
- 1/2 teaspoon salt
- 1/4 cup all-purpose flour
- 2 eggs
- 2 cups sour cream
- 3/4 teaspoon vanilla
- 1 graham cracker pie shell (9 inches), unbaked
- 1 can blueberry pie filling
- 1 cup whipped cream

In a mixing bowl, combine the first six ingredients and mix well. Pour into the pie shell and bake in a preheated, 350° oven for 30 minutes, or until the center is set. Top hot pie with blueberry filling. Chill several hours. When ready to serve, top with whipped cream. **Yield:** 1 pie.

CRAB IMPERIAL

- 1 pound crabmeat (fresh is best—pick through to remove cartilage)
- 2 stalks celery, minced
- 1/3 cup mayonnaise
- 1 teaspoon fresh lemon juice
- 1/4 teaspoon salt
- 1/4 teaspoon Accent
- 2 dashes Worcestershire sauce
- 1/2 teaspoon granulated garlic

Cracker crumbs
Parmesan cheese
Butter

Butter casserole dish. Combine all ingredients except cracker crumbs and cheese in a bowl. Mix well, then let sit for 1 hour. Place in the buttered casserole dish. Top with cracker crumbs and Parmesan cheese, and dot with butter. Bake in a 350° oven for 20 minutes. **Yield:** 4 servings.

STUFFED CORNISH GAME HENS SUPREME WITH WILD RICE

- 2 Cornish hens
- 1/2 bunch scallions, chopped
- 1/2 cup fresh mushrooms, chopped
- 1 cup prepared bread crumbs
- 1/3 cup sour cream
- 1 hard boiled egg (chopped)

Salt and pepper

Garlic butter

SUPREME SAUCE
Drippings from hens
- 1/2 cup butter
- 1/4 cup scallions (chopped)
- 1/2 cup fresh mushrooms (sliced)
- 1/2 cup flour

Milk
Salt and pepper
- 1/2 teaspoon granulated garlic
- 1/2 teaspoon nutmeg
- 1 package wild rice, cooked according to directions

Clean and rinse birds. Mix scallions, mushrooms, bread crumbs, sour cream and egg together in bowl. Gently stuff birds, being sure not to pack stuffing too tightly. Salt and pepper birds. Apply garlic butter to outside of birds. Place breast side up in flat baking dish. Cover dish with aluminum foil and bake in 350° oven for 45 minutes. At the end of the cooking time, remove the foil, drain the drippings and put birds back in oven to brown. SAUCE: Combine the drippings and butter in a small saute pan. Saute scallions and mushrooms until tender. Add flour and stir until a paste is formed. Add milk until desired sauce consistency. Cook wild rice according to package directions. Serve hens on bed of wild rice with Supreme Sauce over the top. **Yield:** Serves 2-4.

NAVY BEAN SOUP

- 1 pound dried navy beans
- 2 tablespoons salt
- 5 cups water
- 1 can (10-3/4-oz.) beef consomme
- 1 chicken bouillon cube
- 4 potatoes, peeled and diced
- 2 onions, diced
- 1/4 cup butter
- 4 carrots, sliced
- 2 cups chopped ham
- 3 bay leaves

Salt and pepper to taste

Rinse beans; place in large kettle. Cover with water, add salt and soak overnight. Drain. Add 5 cups water, consomme and bouillon cube. Bring to a boil and simmer 2 hours. Add potatoes. Saute onions in butter until limp but not brown. Add to soup with remaining ingredients. Add more water if needed. Simmer until vegetables are done. Serve with fresh bread and a green salad. **Yield:** 8 servings.

Best Cook

Meandering with "one foot always in the kitchen" has taken Kathleen Trepp of Huntington Beach, California along some interesting routes.

One of the people she encountered on her way was Nancy Ann Lassater, who worked with Kathleen at a bed and breakfast in Seal Beach, California, and nominated her as "Best Cook in the Country".

"Her recipes are of her own creation, and have won local and state awards," Nancy wrote. "She uses only the finest ingredients, her food presentation is creative and artistic, and the aroma of her creations is reminiscent of grandma's house.

"Most importantly, she is someone I truly admire. She lets me help her, never criticizing or making fun of me for being the ultimate 'non-cook'."

Food has played a large part in Kathleen's life and in her work as owner of a cooking school and in restaurants and inns. She's currently working for a friend in San Pedro, California, in a restaurant called The Grand House, and they've just opened a British pub-style restaurant. As she puts it, "For someone who loves people and entertaining, and who loves to cook and decorate, this kind of work is undeniably the answer to a dream!"

ZUCCHINI PANCAKES

4 medium zucchini, shredded
1/2 medium onion, chopped
1 clove garlic, minced
1/3 cup crumbled feta cheese
2 egg yolks, lightly beaten
1/2 teaspoon salt
1/4 teaspoon pepper
2 tablespoons flour

2 tablespoons olive oil

Shred the zucchini and either work quickly and fry the pancakes immediately or allow the zucchini to drain in a strainer and wring out in a towel to dry. Combine the squash with onion, garlic, egg yolks, cheese, salt and pepper and flour. Heat oil in a large skillet; drop zucchini mixture by 1 tablespoon portions into the hot oil. Fry for a minute; turn and fry other side. (Pancakes may be held at room temperature and warmed before serving or can be frozen.) **Yield: 6 to 8 servings.**

WHITE GAZPACHO

3 peeled cucumbers, cut in chunks
2 cups chicken broth
1 pint sour cream *or* plain yogurt
1 clove garlic
1-1/2 teaspoons salt
1-1/2 tablespoons white wine vinegar

Combine all ingredients and mix in blender. Let stand overnight. When serving, garnish with avocado, bell pepper, toasted almonds and peeled and seeded tomatoes. **Yield: 8 cups.**

BAKED EGGS GRUYERE IN SHELLS

4 slices bacon, cut into 1/2-inch strips
3/4 cup (3 ounces) shredded Gruyere *or* Swiss cheese
4 large eggs
4 teaspoons whipping cream
Salt and pepper

In a 6- to 8-in. frying pan, cook bacon over medium heat until crisp; drain on paper towels. Brush four scallop shells or four 6- to 8-oz. ramekins generously with some of the bacon fat. Sprinkle 1-1/2 tablespoons of cheese over the bottom of each shell; sprinkle on equal portions of bacon. Break one egg into each shell. Pour 1 teaspoon cream over each egg; sprinkle lightly with salt and pepper and equal portions of the remaining cheese. Bake, uncovered, at 350° until set to your liking—12 to 14 minutes for soft yolks. (Eggs continue to cook slightly after coming out of oven.) **Yield: 4 servings.**

FRENCH FRUIT PIES

Pate Brisee (makes dough for 2 pies):
3 cups all-purpose flour
Salt to taste
2 sticks butter
1/3 cup ice water

Filling (enough for one pie):
About 3 cups fresh sliced fruit—plums, peaches, nectarines
1/2 cup heavy whipping cream
1/2 cup sugar
2 eggs
Confectioners' sugar

Put flour and salt in large mixing bowl; cut in butter until dough resembles cornmeal. Add ice water; mix lightly until dough begins to form a ball. Form into two balls. *Do not overhandle.* Let dough rest for at least 20 minutes. (Dough can be stored in refrigerator for a week before being used.) Roll out as for pie crust. Line two 10-1/2-in. tart pans (with removable bottoms) with dough. Fill each crust with sliced fruit; add mixture of cream, sugar and eggs, pouring over fruit. Bake at 350° for 30-35 minutes. Remove from oven; dust with confectioners' sugar. **Yield: 2 pies.**

LIMA BEAN PUREE: In a saucepan, combine two 10-oz. packages of frozen small lima beans with 1 teaspoon salt and enough water to cover. Bring to a boil and simmer 5 minutes. Drain. Puree the beans in a blender or food processor with 2 tablespoons butter, 3 tablespoons sour cream and salt and pepper to taste. **Yield: 4 to 6 servings.**

MOUTH-WATERING MAIN DISHES!
Clockwise from lower left—**Chalupa**, Gail Koehn, Dalhart, Texas (Pg. 27); **Shredded Barbecued Beef**, Carol Wilson, Shingletown, California (Pg. 27); **One-Dish Meal**, Ina Hooper, Elizabeth, Louisiana (Pg. 27); **Spiced Lentil Soup**, Marty Rummel, Trout Lake, Washington (Pg. 28); **Chinese Cashew Chicken**, Pamela Friesen, Lemon Grove, California (Pg. 28); **Apples, Sauerkraut and Chops**, Lois Fetting, Nelson, Wisconsin (Pg. 28); **Three-Alarm Chili**, Lorie Pfeifer, Medicine Hat, Alberta (Pg. 27); **Chicken Parisienne**, Caryn Wiggins, Columbus, Indiana (Pg. 27).

Here's to carefree cooking, the kind that tends to its tasty self while you pitch in with outdoor chores.

These simple, slow-cooking main dish meals don't stint on stick-to-your-ribs goodness. Each features a filling blend of well-seasoned meats and vegetables, in flavors to please every palate.

Enjoy hearty bean and sausage dishes...Old World pork and kraut casseroles...standby soups and stews. This is eating that appetites applaud!

Turn to these recipes the next time you need a substantial field lunch, a delectable dish to pass or a mainstay meal that cooks while the cook's away. All were family kitchen-tested and won "second helping, please" praise from everyone who tasted them. So don't be slow in trying them at your table!

♥

What could be more delicious than a dinner simmered all day to its savory best? Just imagine the aroma of these slow-cooking favorites greeting you as you come in the door! Add some freshly sliced bread...the beverage of your choice...and get ready to dig in to a meal that satisfies.

SAVORY SLOW COOKERS: Clockwise from top—**Chicken Cacciatore**, Aggie Arnold-Norman, Liberty, Pennsylvania (Pg. 28); **Gone-All-Day Stew**, Patty Kile, Plymouth Meeting, Pennsylvania (Pg. 28); **Big Red Soup**, Shelly Korell, Bayard, Nebraska (Pg. 28); **Kapuzta**, Liz Korcak, Montgomery, Minnesota (Pg. 29).

Recipes from Amy Kraemer, Hutchinson, Minnesota.

meals in MINUTES

FISHING for new ideas for fast food? Try this speedy sea-fare menu. It's tasty, nutritious, and ready in 30 minutes!

This good, wholesome menu is great when you have a taste for fish. Oven-frying is a fast but flavorful way of preparing fish fillets. And there's a healthy bonus—oven frying uses much less oil than pan-frying. Any kind of firm white fish, either fresh or frozen, works well in this recipe. The equally prompt potato side dish can be cooked at the same time.

The colorful salad contains some usual and unusual ingredients. Jicama (pronounced HEE-kah-mah) shines as a salad ingredient. Its crunchy texture will remind you of water chestnut. This tuberous vegetable is also a fine addition to marinated mixed vegetable salads, because of the way it keeps its crunch. Jicama is available year-round, and is as tasty boiled, fried or steamed as it is raw in salads.

If you're really rushed, use a purchased Italian oil and vinegar dressing instead of homemade.

OVEN-FRIED FISH

1/4 cup butter, melted
1-1/2 tablespoons lemon juice
1/2 teaspoon sugar
1/4 teaspoon pepper
1/4 teaspoon paprika
1/4 teaspoon basil
1/8 teaspoon garlic powder
1/2 teaspoon salt
1 pound firm fish fillets (cod or haddock), cut in serving pieces
1/3 cup dry bread crumbs
Vegetable oil

Combine butter, lemon juice, sugar and spices. Dip fish in butter/herb mixture; roll in the bread crumbs. Spread enough oil to lightly coat shallow glass baking dish; arrange fish in single layer. Spoon the remaining butter/herb mixture over fish. Bake, uncovered, at 450° for 15 minutes, or until fish flakes easily with fork. **Yield:** 3-4 servings.

IDAHO OVEN FRIES

5 medium baking potatoes, scrubbed, unpeeled
4 tablespoons *melted* butter OR vegetable oil
Salt, pepper to taste

Slice potatoes into 1/8-in. to 1/16-in. thickness and place in ice water. Drain; pat dry with paper towels. Pour melted butter or oil on large baking sheet. Add potato slices to pan, turning to coat with the butter/oil. Season, if desired. Bake at 450° for 15 minutes or until potatoes are tender. **Yield:** 4 servings.

ORANGE/JICAMA SALAD

DRESSING:
4 tablespoons white vinegar
4 tablespoons oil
1/4 teaspoon paprika
1/4 teaspoon salt
1/4 teaspoon white pepper
1 clove garlic, minced
2 teaspoons sugar

SALAD:
4 seedless oranges, peeled and cut in small chunks
1 medium sweet green pepper, seeded
1 small jicama OR 4-6 water chestnuts, peeled and sliced

Make dressing; shake well in covered container. Set aside. Cut pepper into 2-in. x 1/4-in. pieces. Layer oranges, peppers and jicama in bowl; pour dressing over all before serving.

CHOCOLATE WAFER DESSERT

4 servings.

1 pint chocolate ice cream
6 ice cream wafers

Put scoops of ice cream in glass bowls. Stick wafers at angles in ice cream. **Yield:** 4 servings.

♥ P ussy willows, daf-
fodils and the first robin are all
harbingers of spring, but country
cooks look for more savory signs
—such as the first red strawberries,
leafy spinach, spring "fryer" chickens and garden-fresh asparagus.

Build a springtime celebration
around these brunch recipes—the
handsome Country Brunch dish...
colorful Asparagus Au Gratin...
add crunch and color with two unusual fresh spinach salads...try the
oven-fried chicken breasts or fruit-
based chicken salad...and for a
tasty accompaniment, serve hearty
oat-orange muffins or truly flaky
country biscuits.

SAVORY SPRINGTIME FAVORITES:
Clockwise from lower left—**Spinach
Orange Salad,** LeMae Weiland, Ver-
ona, Wisconsin (Pg. 30); **Country
Brunch,** Katherine Clauson, Perham,
Minnesota (Pg. 30); **Colonel Muncy's
Oven-Fried Chicken,** Estle Muncy,
Jefferson City, Tennessee (Pg. 30);
Flaky Biscuits, Marie Hattrup, The
Dalles, Oregon (Pg. 30); **Oatmeal
Orange Bread/Muffins,** Julianne John-
son, Grove City, Minnesota (Pg. 31); **As-
paragus Au Gratin,** Deanna House,
Portage, Michigan (Pg. 31); **Spring
Strawberry Spinach Salad,** Marilyn
Hency, Tualitin, Oregon (Pg. 31); **Pine-
apple Chicken Salad,** Maxine Wil-
liams, Coulee Dam, Washington (Pg. 30).

For a tart taste of spring, try rhubarb! Known as "pie plant" in grandmother's day, thanks to frequent appearances in pie fillings, rhubarb is still an all-time country favorite.

Rhubarb finds its way into a host of desserts, since the piquant taste of this vegetable-masquerading-as-a-fruit is a perfect contrast for a sweet and crunchy topping...custard filling...melt-in-the-mouth meringue...or moist cake. Give these pie plant favorites a try!

PIE PLANT DESSERTS: Clockwise from lower right—**Rhubarb Crunch**, Florence Rasmussen, Amboy, Illinois (Pg. 31); **Rhubarb Cream Delight**, Judy Jungwirth, Athol, South Dakota (Pg. 32); **Rhubarb Custard Pie**, Veronica Neuhalfen, St. Marys, Kansas (Pg. 32); **Rhubarb Cake**, Nancy Moyer, DeRuyter, New York (Pg. 31).

SHREDDED BARBECUED BEEF
Carol Wilson, Shingletown, California

(PICTURED ON PAGE 20)

5 pounds chuck roast
1/2 cup brown sugar
1/4 cup apple cider vinegar
2 cups water
2-3/4 cups catsup
1 tablespoon dry mustard
1 large onion, chopped
1 to 2 cloves garlic, minced
Sesame buns
Sliced red onion
Grated sharp cheddar cheese

Combine the beef, brown sugar, vinegar and water in 6-qt. cast-iron or other heavy oven-proof pot. Bake at 375° for 3 hours. Remove from oven; cool. Remove all fat and any bones. Shred beef; return to pot. Add mixture of catsup, mustard, onion and garlic; stir to blend. Reduce oven temperature to 300° and cook, covered, for up to 4 hours. Stir every half hour, adding more water/catsup to keep well moistened. Serve on buns with the onion and cheese. **Yield:** 12-14 servings.

ONE-DISH MEAL
Ina Hooper, Elizabeth, Louisiana

(PICTURED ON PAGE 20)

1/2 to 1 pound *lean* ground meat
12 ounces lean bacon, cut in small pieces
1 cup chopped onions
1/2 cup chopped green onions
1/4 cup chopped green pepper
1/2 pound smoked sausage, sliced 1/4 inch thick
1 can (16 ounces) kidney beans, drained
1 can (16 ounces) pork and beans, drained
1 can (16 ounces) lima beans, drained
1 cup cooked soybeans OR Northern white beans, drained
1 cup catsup OR chili sauce
1/4 cup honey or brown sugar
1 tablespoon liquid smoke, *optional*
3 tablespoons white vinegar
1 teaspoon salt
1 tablespoon Worcestershire sauce
Dash red and black pepper

Brown ground beef in skillet (or cook in microwave). Drain off fat; place beef in slow cooker. Brown bacon

pieces; remove to paper towel. Drain fat from skillet; lightly brown onions and green pepper. Add bacon, onions and pepper to slow cooker; stir in remaining ingredients. Cover; cook on low for 4-6 hours. **Yield:** 12 servings.

CHALUPA
Gail Koehn, Dalhart, Texas

(PICTURED ON PAGE 20)

3 pounds pork roast, cut in bite-size pieces
1 pound pinto beans, soaked in water overnight, if desired
3 cloves garlic, chopped
3 teaspoons chili powder
1 teaspoon cumin
1 teaspoon oregano
1 can (4 ounces) chopped green chilies
1 jar (12 ounces) mild chunky salsa
Salt to taste
Corn chips
Shredded cheese
Chopped tomatoes
Shredded lettuce
Taco sauce

Mix first 9 ingredients together; place in slow cooker. Cover with water (reduce water slightly if beans are presoaked). Cover cooker; cook on high for 5 hours. Serve in layers of corn chips, meat mixture, cheese, tomato, lettuce and taco sauce. **Yield:** 15 servings.

✓CHICKEN PARISIENNE
Caryn Wiggins, Columbus, Indiana

(PICTURED ON PAGE 20)

6 medium chicken breast *halves*
Salt
Pepper
Paprika
1/2 teaspoon leaf rosemary, *optional*
1/2 cup dry white wine OR water
1 can (10-3/4 ounces) cream of mushroom soup, *undiluted*
1 can (4 ounces) sliced mushrooms, *drained*
1 cup dairy sour cream
1/4 cup flour

Sprinkle chicken breasts lightly with the salt, pepper, paprika and rosemary, if desired. Place in 3-1/2-qt.

slow cooker. Mix water/wine, soup and mushrooms until well blended. (You may add sour cream/flour mixture now if you will be cooking on *low* temperature.) Pour liquid over chicken breasts in slow cooker. Sprinkle with paprika. Cover; cook on low 6-8 hours. (Or cook on high for 2-1/2 to 3 hours, adding sour cream/flour mixture during last 30 minutes.) Serve chicken and sauce over rice or over noodles. **Yield:** 6 servings. **Diabetic Exchanges:** One serving equals 1/2 bread, 1 vegetable, 1 fat; also, 308 calories, 495 mg sodium, 87 mg cholesterol, 11 gm carbohydrate, 29 gm protein, 16 gm fat.

✓ THREE-ALARM CHILI
Lorie Pfeifer, Medicine Hat, Alberta

(PICTURED ON PAGE 21)

4 tablespoons vegetable oil
2 pounds stewing beef, cut into 1/2-inch cubes
3 medium onions, diced
4 cloves garlic, minced
1 can (28 ounces) whole tomatoes
1 can (16 ounces) tomato sauce
1 cup water
3 tablespoons brown sugar
1 teaspoon oregano
3 tablespoons chili powder
2 teaspoons salt
1/4 teaspoon dried, crushed red pepper
2 cans (16 ounces *each*) kidney beans, drained
1 large green pepper, diced
1 large sweet red pepper, diced

Heat oil in Dutch oven; brown beef on all sides, then remove and drain well on paper towels. Cook onions and garlic in oil; return meat to pan. Add the tomatoes, sauce, water, sugar, oregano, chili powder, salt and crushed red pepper. Bring to boil over high heat. Reduce heat; simmer 1-1/2 hours. Add remaining three ingredients. Simmer, covered, until meat is tender. **Yield:** 12 servings. **Diabetic Exchanges** One serving equals 2 protein, 1 bread, 2 vegetable, 1 fat; also, 289 calories, 746 mg sodium, 69 mg cholesterol, 26 gm carbohydrate, 23 gm protein, 11 gm fat.

SPICED LENTIL SOUP

Marty Rummel, Trout Lake, Washington

(PICTURED ON PAGE 21)

1/2 pound Italian sausage, crumbled, casing removed
1/2 cup diced onion
1/3 cup barley
3 cloves garlic
3 quarts chicken stock
1 cup lentils
1 whole chicken breast, uncooked
1/2 cup parsley, chopped
1 can (15 ounces) garbanzo beans and juice
1/2 to 1 pound fresh OR frozen spinach
1 jar (12 ounces) mild to medium salsa

Brown sausage, onion, barley and garlic together in skillet. Remove and place in bottom of slow cooker or large stock pot. Add the chicken stock, lentils, uncooked chicken breast and parsley. Simmer for as long as you desire or until lentils are tender. Remove chicken breast, discarding bone and cartilage. Shred meat and return to cooker. Add beans, spinach and salsa to soup mixture; heat through. Serve with hot biscuits or muffins. **Yield:** 10 servings.

APPLES, SAUERKRAUT AND CHOPS

Lois Fetting, Nelson, Wisconsin

(PICTURED ON PAGE 21)

4 pork chops, cut 1/2 inch thick, trimmed
Vegetable oil for browning
1 medium onion, sliced, separated into rings
1/8 teaspoon *instant* garlic flakes
3 cups *drained* sauerkraut
3/4 cup apple juice
1-1/2 teaspoons caraway seed
1/4 teaspoon salt
1/4 teaspoon thyme
1/4 teaspoon pepper
1 cup apple slices, unpeeled, cored *red cooking variety*

Brown pork chops in nonstick pan; set aside. (Omit this step if in a hurry.) Place in a slow cooker *half* of onion rings, garlic flakes, sauerkraut, apple juice, caraway seed, salt, thyme and pepper. Add pork chops. Place the remaining *half* of ingredi-

ents on top of chops; top with apple slices. Cover slow cooker; cook on low for 6-8 hours or on high for 4 hours. **Yield:** 4 generous servings.

CHINESE CASHEW CHICKEN

Pamela Friesen, Lemon Grove, California

(PICTURED ON PAGE 21)

1 pound bean sprouts
3 tablespoons butter
1/2 cup chopped green onion
1 can (4 ounces) mushroom pieces
1 can (10-3/4 ounces) cream of mushroom soup, *undiluted*
1 cup cooked chicken pieces (can use leftovers)
1 cup bias-cut celery
1 tablespoon soy sauce
1 cup cashew nuts

Mix all ingredients *except cashew nuts* together in slow cooker. Cook, covered, on low for 4-9 hours or on high for 2-3 hours. Stir in cashew nuts; serve with rice or noodles. **Yield:** 6 servings.

✓ CHICKEN CACCIATORE

Aggie Arnold-Norman, Liberty, Pennsylvania

(PICTURED ON PAGE 22)

2 medium onions, thinly sliced
1 2-1/2-pound to 3-pound boiler/fryer chicken, cut in pieces, skinned
2 cloves garlic, minced
1 teaspoon salt
1/4 teaspoon pepper
1 to 2 teaspoons crushed oregano leaves
1/2 teaspoon leaf basil
1 bay leaf
1 can (16 ounces) tomatoes
1 can (8 ounces) tomato sauce
1 can (4 ounces) mushrooms OR 1 cup fresh mushrooms
1/4 cup water OR dry white wine

Place sliced onions in bottom of slow cooker. Add chicken, seasonings, tomatoes, sauce, mushrooms and water/wine. Cover; cook on low for 6-8 hours *or* on high for 3-4 hours. Serve chicken with sauce over hot buttered spaghetti, linguine or vermicelli. **Yield:** 6 servings. **Diabetic Exchanges:** One serving equals 3 protein, 2 vegetable; also, 180 calories, 745 mg sodium, 177 mg cholesterol, 10 gm carbohydrate, 26 gm protein, 4 gm fat.

✓ GONE-ALL-DAY STEW

Patty Kile, Plymouth Meeting, Pennsylvania

(PICTURED ON PAGE 22)

1 can (10-3/4 ounces) tomato soup, undiluted
1 cup water OR red wine
1/4 cup flour
2 pounds beef chuck, cut in 1-inch to 2-inch cubes, fat trimmed
3 medium carrots, cut in 1-inch diagonal slices
6 white boiling onions OR yellow onions, quartered
4 medium potatoes, cut in 1-1/2-inch chunks
1/2 cup celery, cut in 1-inch chunks
12 whole large fresh mushrooms
2 beef bouillon cubes
1 tablespoon Italian herb seasoning mix OR 1 teaspoon *each* leaf oregano, thyme, rosemary
1 bay leaf
3 grinds fresh pepper

Mix together tomato soup, water/wine and flour until smooth; combine with remaining ingredients in covered roasting pan. Bake at 275° for 4-5 hours. When ready to serve, adjust seasoning, if desired. Serve over noodles or with crunchy French bread (to soak up the gravy). Coleslaw is a nice winter accompaniment *or* serve fresh tomatoes on a bed of lettuce in summer. **Yield:** 8 servings. **Diabetic Exchanges:** One serving equal 3 protein, 1 bread, 2 vegetable, 1/2 fat; also, 311 calories, 660 mg sodium, 103 mg cholesterol, 26 gm carbohydrate, 29 gm protein, 10 gm fat.

BIG RED SOUP

Shelly Korell, Bayard, Nebraska

(PICTURED ON PAGE 22)

2 tablespoons vegetable oil
2 pounds beef stew meat, trimmed
3/4 cup chopped onion
2 cloves garlic, minced
2 cans (14-1/2 ounces *each*) tomatoes
1 can (10-1/2 ounces) beef broth
1 can (10-1/2 ounces) chicken broth
1 can (10-3/4 ounces) tomato soup
1/4 cup water
1 teaspoon ground cumin

1 teaspoon chili powder
1 teaspoon salt
1/2 teaspoon lemon pepper
2 teaspoons Worcestershire sauce
1/3 cup mild picante sauce, unsweetened variety
8 corn tortillas, cut into quarters
4 ounces mild cheddar cheese, grated

Heat oil in skillet; brown beef stew meat. Place meat in slow cooker; add remaining ingredients *except for tortillas and cheese*. Cook on low for at least 10 hours. When serving, place enough tortilla quarters in bottom of each bowl to cover. Pour soup over tortilla pieces; sprinkle with the cheese. **Yield:** 10-12 servings.

KAPUZTA

Liz Krocak, Montgomery, Minnesota

(PICTURED ON PAGE 22)
1-1/2 pounds fresh pork (any type), trimmed, cut in bite-size pieces
1 medium onion, chopped
1-1/2 pounds Polish sausage, sliced in 1/2-inch pieces
1 quart sauerkraut, fresh preferred
1/4 head fresh cabbage, coarsely chopped
1 tablespoon caraway seed
1 can (10-3/4 ounces) cream of mushroom soup
Pepper to taste

Brown pork and onion in hot skillet until pork is cooked through, about 10 minutes. Combine cooked pork and onion with all other ingredients in 5-qt. Dutch oven or slow cooker. Mix lightly; simmer all day. (The longer you cook this, the better it tastes.) **Yield:** 6-8 servings.

BROCCOLI/CHEESE SOUP

Mrs. Roy Hochstetler, West Salem, Ohio

2 cups *cooked* noodles
1 package (10 ounces) frozen chopped broccoli, *thawed*
3 tablespoons chopped onion
2 tablespoons butter
1 tablespoon flour
2 cups cubed processed cheese
Salt to taste
5-1/2 cups milk

Combine all ingredients in slow cooker; stir to blend. Cook on low for 4 hours. **Yield:** 8 servings.

ITALIAN BEEF AU JUS

Jean Moeller, Pipestone, Minnesota

3 to 5 pounds thawed boneless beef roast
SAUCE:
1 package (10 ounces) Au Jus Mix
1 package (.7 ounce) Italian salad dressing mix
1 can (10-1/2 ounces) beef broth
1/2 soup can water

Place beef roast in slow cooker; combine sauce ingredients and pour over beef. Cover; cook on low for 8 hours. Meat may be sliced and served with hard rolls *or* shredded with two forks and served over noodles or rice, with broth thickened with flour. **Yield:** 8-10 servings.

QUICK COUNTRY CLAM CHOWDER

Jan Wical, Grundy Center, Iowa

2 cans (10-3/4 ounces) cream of potato soup
1 pint frozen corn, thawed and drained
1 cup sliced carrots
1 can (6-1/2 ounces) minced clams, *drained*
Milk
Seasoning salt

Combine all ingredients except milk in slow cooker. Add milk to desired consistency. Cook on low for 6-8 hours. **Yield:** 8-10 servings.

SLOW COOKER STUFFING

Elmeda Johnson, East Grand Forks, Minnesota

1 cup butter
2 cups chopped celery
1 cup chopped onion
1 teaspoon poultry seasoning
1-1/2 teaspoons leaf sage, crumbled
1/2 teaspoon pepper
1-1/2 teaspoons salt
1 teaspoon leaf thyme, crumbled

2 eggs, beaten
4 cups chicken broth
12 cups dry bread crumbs

Mix butter, celery, onion, spices, eggs and broth together. Add crumbs; stir to blend. Cook in slow cooker on high for 45 minutes; reduce heat to low for 6 hours. (This recipe comes in handy when you run out of oven space at a large family gathering!) **Yield:** 10-12 servings.

SLOW COOKER BAKED APPLES

Ann Leggett, Jackson, Louisiana

6 to 8 medium baking apples, washed, cored, with top third of apple peeled
FILLING:
Raisins
Chopped pecans
Brown sugar
TOPPING:
1 teaspoon cinnamon
1/2 teaspoon nutmeg
2 tablespoons butter
1/2 cup water

Place apples in slow cooker; fill with raisin/pecan/sugar mixture. Sprinkle with topping spices; dot with butter. Add water. Cover; cook on low for 8 hours or overnight. Delicious for breakfast. **Yield:** 6-8 servings.

SLOW COOKER ITALIAN SAUSAGE

Mildred Rudolph, Hebron, Ohio

2 to 3 pounds mild Italian link sausage
Water
1 large onion, sliced
1 large green pepper, sliced
1 jar (48 ounces) spaghetti sauce

Place sausage in skillet; add water to cover. Bring to boil; cook 10 minutes. Drain. Add sausage to cooker; arrange onion and pepper on top; pour spaghetti sauce over all. Cover; cook on low for 6-8 hours. **Yield:** 4-6 servings.

SLOW-COOKING TIPS: If there's too much liquid in your cooker, stick a toothpick under the edge of the lid to allow steam to escape. • Put vegetables into the pot first to form a rack for the meat. • Add liquids and sauces last to moisten the surfaces of vegetables and meat.

SLOW COOKER PHEASANT (GAME)

Joan Norman, Bloomfield, Iowa

1 pheasant, cleaned, washed and cut in pieces as a fryer*
Flour
Salt to taste
Pepper to taste
   1/2 cup butter
   2 onions, thinly sliced
   1/2 cup water

*Any other small game birds, such as quail, may be used instead of pheasant. Flour pheasant lightly; sprinkle with salt and pepper. Slice half of butter into bottom of slow cooker; cover with thin layer of onions. Arrange pheasant pieces over onion; cover with the remaining onions. Dot with remaining butter. Add water. Cover and cook on low or at 250° for 4-5 hours. **Yield:** 6-8 servings.

SPINACH ORANGE SALAD

LeMae Weiland, Verona, Wisconsin

(PICTURED ON PAGE 24)

DRESSING:
   1/4 cup vegetable oil
   2 tablespoons white sugar
   2 tablespoons white vinegar
   1 tablespoon snipped parsley
   1/2 teaspoon salt
   1/4 teaspoon black pepper
Dash Tabasco sauce
   1/4 cup sliced almonds
   4 teaspoons white sugar
Fresh spinach, washed, dried and chilled (enough for 6-8 people)
   1 cup thin bias-cut celery
   2 tablespoons chopped green onion tops
   1 can (11 ounces) mandarin oranges, drained

Combine dressing ingredients; cover. Shake well and refrigerate. Place almonds and sugar in small skillet. Stir over medium heat *watching closely* until almonds are golden brown.

Remove to small bowl; cool. Place spinach in large salad bowl. Add celery, green onion and oranges. At serving time, add dressing and almonds; toss lightly. **Yield:** 6-8 servings.

PINEAPPLE CHICKEN SALAD

Maxine Williams, Coulee Dam, Washington

(PICTURED ON PAGE 24)
   1/2 cup mayonnaise OR salad dressing
   2 teaspoons prepared mustard
   2 cups (12 ounces) cooked chicken, shredded
   1/2 cup thinly sliced celery
   1 tablespoon *finely* chopped onion
   1/2 cup sliced fresh mushrooms
   1/4 cup chopped green pepper
   1/4 cup sliced pitted ripe olives
   1 can (20 ounces) pineapple chunks OR tidbits*, drained
   1 can (11 ounces) mandarin orange sections*, drained
Lettuce leaves
Croutons, optional

*Refrigerate drained fruits the night before for a well-chilled salad. In medium mixing bowl, stir together mayonnaise and prepared mustard. Stir in chicken, celery, onion, mushrooms, pepper and olives. Cover; refrigerate for several hours. Just before serving, add drained fruit. Serve on lettuce-lined plates; top with croutons, if desired. **Yield:** 6 servings.

FLAKY BISCUITS

Marie Hattrup, The Dalles, Oregon

(PICTURED ON PAGE 24)
   2 cups sifted unbleached flour
   4 teaspoons baking powder
   3 tablespoons sugar
   1/2 teaspoon salt
   1/2 teaspoon cream of tartar
   1/2 cup butter, chilled
   3/4 cup milk, room temperature

Sift together into large mixing bowl—flour, baking powder, sugar, salt and cream of tartar. Cut in butter until bits of butter are the size of medium peas. Mix in milk, only until ingredients are blended. *Do not overmix.* Form into a ball; pat out on floured board to 3/4-in. thickness. Cut into biscuits using a 2-1/2-in. biscuit cutter. Place on ungreased cookie sheet

or in 13-in. x 9-in. x 2-in. pan. Bake at 475° for 10 minutes or until golden brown. **Yield:** 10 biscuits.

BISCUIT BONUS: To ensure biscuits that rise evenly in the oven, use a straight up-and-down motion when cutting. • Before baking refrigerated "canned" biscuits, microwave on HIGH for 1-1/2 to 2 minutes; then complete baking in conventional oven. This yields higher, more moist biscuits.

COLONEL MUNCY'S OVEN-FRIED CHICKEN

Estle Muncy, Jefferson City, Tennessee

(PICTURED ON PAGE 24)
   10 (24 ounces) chicken breasts
   2 cups dairy sour cream OR plain yogurt
   1/4 cup lemon juice
   4 teaspoons Worcestershire sauce
   2 teaspoons celery salt OR ground celery seed
   2 teaspoons paprika
   4 garlic cloves, chopped fine OR 1/2 teaspoon garlic powder
   2 teaspoons salt
   1/2 teaspoon pepper
   2 teaspoons poultry seasoning
   2 teaspoons parsley
   1/2 cup melted margarine
Corn flake crumbs

Cut chicken breasts in half. Wipe dry; remove skin and excess fat. In large bowl, combine all ingredients except margarine and corn flakes; stir well. Add chicken, making sure each piece is covered well. Let stand overnight in refrigerator. Remove chicken pieces from mixture; blot off excess with dry towel. Dip each piece in melted margarine, then roll in corn flake crumbs. Place chicken in single layer on shallow baking pan. Sprinkle with additional parsley. Bake at 375° for 25-30 minutes or until chicken tests done. **Yield:** 10 servings.

COUNTRY BRUNCH

Katherine Clauson, Perham, Minnesota

(PICTURED ON PAGE 24)
   16 slices firm white bread
2-1/2 cups cooked, cubed ham, about 1 pound

16 ounces cheddar cheese,
shredded
16 ounces mozzarella cheese,
shredded
6 eggs
3 cups whole milk
1/2 teaspoon dry mustard
1/8 to 1/4 teaspoon onion powder

TOPPING:
3 cups *uncrushed* corn flakes
1/2 cup butter, melted

Trim crusts from bread; cut slices in half. Grease a 13-in. x 9-in. x 2-in. baking pan and layer as follows: Cover bottom of pan with one-half of bread, one-half of ham and one-half of each of the cheeses. Repeat layers. Combine eggs, milk and seasonings. Pour over layers; refrigerate overnight. Remove from refrigerator 30 minutes before baking. Combine topping ingredients; sprinkle over casserole. Bake at 375° for 45 minutes (cover loosely with foil to prevent top from over-browning). Let stand 10-15 minutes before cutting into squares. **Yield:** 12-15 servings.

ASPARAGUS AU GRATIN
Deanna House, Portage, Michigan

(PICTURED ON PAGE 25)
1-1/4 pounds fresh asparagus Or 1 (10 ounces) package frozen asparagus
2 tablespoons butter OR margarine
2 tablespoons chopped onion
2 tablespoons flour
1/2 teaspoon salt
1/8 teaspoon ground white pepper
Dash of ground nutmeg OR mace
2/3 cup chicken broth
1/3 cup half-and-half coffee cream
Toast points, rusks OR Texas toast
Butter OR margarine
1/2 cup (2 ounces) shredded cheddar cheese

Clean and cook asparagus in small amount of boiling water (or microwave) until tender crisp, about 3-

4 minutes. Drain; set aside. In medium saucepan, melt butter; stir in onion; cook until transparent. Stir in flour, salt, pepper and nutmeg/mace over low heat until smooth. Stir in broth and cream; cook until thickened, stirring constantly. Set aside. Butter Texas toast, rusks or toast points; place under preheated broiler until golden brown. Remove to 13-in. x 9-in. x 2-in. baking dish. Place asparagus over bread; pour sauce over all. Sprinkle with cheese. Bake at 400° for 8-10 minutes until cheese melts. **Yield:** 4 servings.

SPRING STRAWBERRY SPINACH SALAD
Marilyn Hency, Tualatin, Oregon

(PICTURED ON PAGE 25)
10 large firm strawberries
1 large bunch spinach

DRESSING:
1/2 cup sugar
1 teaspoon salt
1 teaspoon dry mustard
1/3 cup white wine OR white vinegar
1 cup vegetable oil
1 tablespoon (rounded) poppy seeds

Wash, drain and tear spinach into serving-size pieces. Place in large salad bowl; chill. Slice strawberries in half (may also leave whole, if desired). Set aside. Mix dressing ingredients (except poppy seeds) together in blender. Stir in poppy seeds. Just before serving, mix dressing with spinach and reserved strawberries. **Yield:** 4-5 servings.

OATMEAL ORANGE BREAD/MUFFINS
Julianne Johnson, Grove City, Minnesota

(PICTURED ON PAGE 25)
2 cups all-purpose flour
3/4 cup sugar
4-1/2 teaspoons baking powder
1/2 teaspoon baking soda
1/2 teaspoon salt
1-1/2 cups rolled oats
1 orange *rind and sections*
2 eggs, beaten
2 tablespoons butter, melted
1 cup water

Stir together flour, sugar, baking powder, soda, salt and oats; set aside. Mix in 1 tablespoon of addi-

tional sugar with grated orange rind and *diced* sections; set aside. Combine beaten eggs with butter, orange mixture and water. Combine with dry ingredients; stir to blend. Pour into a 1-1/2-qt. greased casserole, 9-in. greased loaf pan or greased muffin tins. Bake casserole or loaf at 350° for 45-55 minutes; muffins for 30 minutes.

RHUBARB CRUNCH
Florence Rasmussen, Amboy, Illinois

(PICTURED ON PAGE 26)
3 cups diced rhubarb
1 cup sugar
3 tablespoons flour

TOPPING:
1 cup brown sugar
1 cup old-fashioned rolled oats
1-1/2 cups flour
1/2 cup butter
1/2 cup vegetable shortening

Combine rhubarb, sugar and flour; place in greased 13-in x 9-in. x 2-in. pan. Combine brown sugar, oats and flour; cut in butter and shortening until crumbly. Sprinkle over rhubarb mixture. Bake at 375° for 40 minutes. Serve warm with ice cream, whipped cream or milk. **Yield:** 10-12 servings.

RHUBARB CAKE
Nancy Moyer, DeRuyter, New York

(PICTURED ON PAGE 26)
1/2 cup softened butter
1-1/2 cups sugar
1 egg
1 cup buttermilk
2 cups flour, unsifted (reserve 2 tablespoons to mix with rhubarb)
1 teaspoon baking soda
1/2 teaspoon salt
1 teaspoon cinnamon
2 cups diced rhubarb, fresh OR frozen

Cream together butter, sugar and egg; add buttermilk alternately with combined flour, soda, salt and cinnamon. Mix until smooth. Add vanilla. Toss rhubarb with flour, add to mixture; spread in greased and floured 13-in. x 9-in. x 2-in. cake pan. Bake at 350° for 35 minutes. Serve plain or with whipped cream.

RHUBARB CUSTARD PIE
Veronica Nuehalfen, St. Marys, Kansas

(PICTURED ON PAGE 26)
3 cups rhubarb, partially peeled, cut in 1/4-inch pieces
3 tablespoons flour, well-rounded
1 cup sugar
1 9-inch *unbaked* pie shell
3 eggs, separated
1 tablespoon thick dairy sour cream

TOPPING:
1-1/2 cups old-fashioned OR quick-cooking oats
1 cup brown sugar
1/2 teaspoon cinnamon
1/4 cup butter OR margarine

Place cut rhubarb in large mixing bowl; combine flour and sugar. Add to rhubarb, mix and let stand while preparing the crust. Using your favorite pastry recipe for a single crust pie, make a pie shell with a high fluted edge in order to hold all of the topping. Brush the bottom and sides of crust with egg white from separated egg (prevents crust from becoming soggy). Beat egg yolks and sour cream until thick; add to rhubarb mixture. Pour into pie shell. Combine topping ingredients; spread evenly over pie. Bake at 400° for 10 minutes; reduce heat to 350°; bake 50 minutes more.

RHUBARB CREAM DELIGHT
Judy Jungwirth, Athol, South Dakota

(PICTURED ON PAGE 26)
CRUST:
1-1/2 cups flour
3 tablespoons sugar
3/4 cup butter OR margarine
CREAM FILLING:
2 cups sugar
4 egg yolks, beaten
2/3 cup cream OR evaporated milk
3 tablespoons flour
1/2 teaspoon nutmeg
4 cups chopped rhubarb
MERINGUE:
4 egg whites
1/4 cup sugar

Combine crust ingredients until crumbly; press into a 13-in. x 9-in. x 2-in. baking pan. Bake at 350° for 20 minutes. While crust is baking, com-bine all filling ingredients and cook in *heavy* saucepan over medium heat. Stir constantly until thickened—watch carefully because mixture will scorch easily. (Mixture may also be cooked in microwave.) Pour hot filling into crust; top with meringue made by beating egg whites with sugar until thick and satiny. Bake at 325° for 15-20 minutes or until golden brown. Refrigerate any leftovers. **Yield: 10-12 servings.**

BAKED EGGPLANT CASSEROLE
Rowena Champagne, New Iberia, Louisiana

2 medium eggplants, peeled, cut in 1-inch cubes
1 stick butter, *divided*
1/2 pound chopped ham
1 pound peeled, raw shrimp
2 cups chopped onions
1 cup chopped green peppers
1 cup chopped green onions
1 cup seasoned Italian bread crumbs
Parmesan cheese

Steam eggplant in water until tender (approximately 15 minutes). Drain and set aside. Melt 3 tablespoons butter in large skillet; add ham and shrimp. Cook over medium heat for about 7 minutes or until shrimp turns pink. Remove from skillet; set aside. Saute onions, peppers and green onions in remaining butter until vegetables are tender; stir in eggplant, ham and shrimp. Pour into buttered 2-qt. casserole; sprinkle with mixture of bread crumbs and cheese. Bake, uncovered, at 325° for about 20 minutes. **Yield: 8 servings.**

BUTTERMILK PECAN PIE
Laura Julian, Littleton, New Hampshire

1/2 cup margarine, softened
2 cups sugar
2 teaspoons vanilla
3 eggs
1/4 cup all-purpose flour
1/4 teaspoon salt
1 cup buttermilk
3/4 cup chopped pecans
One 9 or 10-inch unbaked pie shell

Cream margarine and sugar. Blend in vanilla, then eggs, one at a time, beating after each addition. Gradually beat in flour and salt; add buttermilk. Set aside. Sprinkle pecans in pie shell; pour in filling. Bake at 300° for 1-1/2 hours. Cool before cutting. May be served warm or cold. Refrigerate leftovers. **Yield: 8 servings.**

AMISH SUGAR COOKIES
Sylvia Ford, Kennett, Missouri

1 cup margarine, unsalted, softened
1 cup corn oil
1 cup granulated sugar
1 cup confectioners' sugar
2 eggs
1 teaspoon vanilla
4-1/2 cups all-purpose flour
1 teaspoon baking soda
1 teaspoon cream of tartar

Combine margarine, oil and sugars in large mixing bowl; mix well. Add eggs; beat 1 minute. Add vanilla; mix well. Add flour, baking soda and cream of tartar; combine until smooth. Drop by small teaspoons on ungreased cookie sheet. Bake at 375° for 8-10 minutes. Cool on wire rack. **Yield: 4 dozen cookies.**

CHICKEN BROCCOLI CASSEROLE
Irene Conrad, Marion, Indiana

3 chicken breasts, skinned and boned
1 teaspoon salt
2 teaspoons leaf marjoram, crumbled
1/2 cup chopped celery
1 package (8 ounces) frozen chopped broccoli (thawed)
2 teaspoons butter
1 can (4 ounces) sliced mushrooms
1 small can water chestnuts, drained
SAUCE:
1 cup creamy salad dressing
2 teaspoons prepared mustard
1 can (10-3/4 ounces) cream of mushroom soup
1/2 teaspoon lemon juice
1/2 teaspoon curry powder
TOPPING:
1 cup grated cheddar cheese
1/4 cup Parmesan cheese
1/2 cup fine buttered bread crumbs

Poach chicken breasts (or cook in microwave) in water to cover, salt, marjoram and celery until tender. Remove chicken; discard cooking liquid. Cool; cut or tear chicken into strips. Place in bottom of 2-1/2 quart casserole. Cover with broccoli, dot with butter. Add drained mushrooms and water chestnuts; set aside. Combine sauce ingredients in small bowl; pour over chicken/broccoli. Sprinkle top with cheddar cheese; combine bread crumbs and Parmesan cheese; sprinkle evenly over top. Bake at 350° for about 30 minutes. **Yield:** 10 servings.

CHICKEN RICE PIE

Trudy Selberg, Rogers, Arkansas

CRUST:
    2 cups *cooked* parboiled long grain rice
    1/2 cup cooked chopped spinach, well drained
    1 cup grated Swiss cheese

FILLING:
    1 can (10-3/4 ounces) cream of mushroom soup, *undiluted*
    1/2 cup milk
    2 cups cooked, cubed chicken
    1 cup mild grated cheddar cheese
    1/2 cup Parmesan cheese
    2 ounces green olives, sliced
    1/4 cup onion, finely chopped
    1/2 cup fresh mushrooms, sliced

Combine crust ingredients; spray 10-inch pie pan with vegetable spray. Press crust onto bottom and sides of pan. Bake at 375° for 25 minutes. Set aside. Combine soup and milk; mixing well. Add remaining filling ingredients; mix gently. Spread mixture over cooked crust. Bake, uncovered, at 350° for 20-25 minutes. Remove from oven; let stand 10 minutes before serving. **Yield:** 6-8 servings.

✓BARBECUED BANANAS

Iris Bates, Midhurst, Ontario

    6 bananas
    1/4 cup fresh lemon juice
    2 tablespoons brown sugar
    1/4 teaspoon cinnamon
    1/4 teaspoon nutmeg
    1/8 teaspoon mace
    3 tablespoons butter

Peel bananas; place on double thickness of heavy-duty foil. Brush with lemon juice; sprinkle with sugar and spices. Dot with butter. Wrap, sealing

tightly. Barbecue on grill for 9-10 minutes; unwrap carefully. Eat with a spoon. **Yield:** 6 servings. **Diabetic Exchanges:** One serving equals 3 fruits, 1 fat; also 166 calories, 72 mg sodium, 18 mg cholesterol, 30 gm carbohydrates.

SAUSAGE/WILD RICE CASSEROLE

Charlene Griffin, Minocqua, Wisconsin

    1 pound bulk pork sausage
    1/2 cup celery, chopped
    1 tablespoon dried green pepper flakes
    1 can (10-3/4 ounces) cream of mushroom soup, *undiluted*
    1-1/2 cups water
    1 cup wild rice, uncooked
    1 jar (4 ounces) diced pimiento, drained
    1 jar (2-1/2 ounces) sliced mushrooms, drained
    1 cup (4 ounces) shredded cheddar cheese
    1 tablespoon instant minced onion
    2 teaspoons dried leaf marjoram, crumbled
    1 teaspoon dried leaf thyme

Brown sausage in Dutch oven; stirring to crumble. Add celery, pepper flakes; saute until celery is tender. Drain off pan drippings. Stir in soup, water, wild rice, pimiento, mushrooms, cheese, onion, marjoram and thyme. Pour into a lightly greased 12-in. x 8-in. x 2-in. baking dish. Cover; bake at 350° for 1-1/2 hours or until rice is tender. **Yield:** 8 servings.

PRUNE CAKE

Lucille Drake, Tecumseh, Michigan

    1 cup vegetable oil
    1-1/2 cups granulated sugar
    3 eggs
    2 cups all-purpose flour
    1 teaspoon cinnamon
    1 teaspoon nutmeg
    1 teaspoon allspice

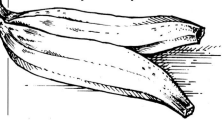

    1 teaspoon baking soda
    1 cup buttermilk
    1 teaspoon vanilla
    2 cups prunes, cooked, seeded and chopped
    1 cup nuts

Beat oil and sugar until well blended; add eggs, one at a time, beating after each addition. Combine dry ingredients; add alternately with buttermilk and vanilla to creamed mixture; beating until smooth. Stir in prunes and nuts. Pour into a greased 13-in. x 9-in. x 2-in. baking pan. Bake at 300° for 45 minutes. Cool. Dust with confectioners' sugar or frost with favorite cream cheese icing, if desired. **Yield:** 16-20 servings.

MISSISSIPPI MUD PIE

Sara W. Carley, Temple, New Hampshire

(PICTURED ON PAGE 90)
CRUST:
    24 chocolate wafers, mashed fine, about 1-1/3 cups crumbs, *divided*
    3 tablespoons soft butter *or* margarine

FILLING:
    1/2 gallon coffee ice cream, slightly softened

HOT FUDGE SAUCE:
    2 squares unsweetened chocolate
    1/2 cup water
    1-1/2 cups light corn syrup
    1/8 teaspoon salt
    1 teaspoon vanilla extract

WHIPPED CREAM TOPPING:
    1 cup whipping cream
    1 tablespoon sugar
    1 teaspoon vanilla extract

Make the crust by combining crumbs and butter/margarine. Set aside 3 tablespoons of mixture for pie garnish. Press remaining into bottom and sides of 9-in. pie plate. Bake at 375° for 8 minutes; cool. Pack softened ice cream into cooled crust. Freeze until firm. Make fudge sauce by melting chocolate with water in saucepan over low heat until blended. Remove from heat; gradually add syrup and salt. Bring to boil; reduce heat and simmer for 10 minutes, stirring often. Add vanilla. Set aside. Whip cream; add sugar and vanilla. To serve, cut pie into wedges, place on dessert plates, pour fudge sauce over all, top with whipped cream and sprinkle with the reserved crumbs, if desired. **Yield:** 8 servings.

Country Inns

Sonka Sheep Station Inn
901 NW Chadwick Lane
Myrtle Creek, Oregon 97457
503/863-5168

Directions: From Roseburg, follow I-5 south about 20 miles to Exit #103 (Tri City); left on Hwy. 386 about 1-1/2 miles to Chadwick Lane; left to ranch.

Owners: Louis and Evelyn Sonka

Schedule: Open year-round except Christmas holidays.

Rates and Accommodations: 4 rooms with 2 shared baths, $45-$55 double occupancy; full occupancy of 2-bedroom guest house with bath and kitchen, $75/night for 3 or more nights. Advance reservations required. Visa, Master Card. Hours and rates are subject to change. Please call or write.

Bordering the South Umpqua River in southwestern Oregon is Sonka's Sheep Station Inn, situated on a 300-acre working sheep ranch.

The inn features fresh, Oregon-grown country fare. Dinner guests are often offered Greek Lamb Appetizers before a savory dinner of freshly caught salmon or a leg of lamb marinated in herbs and spices, accompanied by fresh asparagus and a spinach salad. Blackberries grow in abundance along the river, so guests are sure to be offered wild blackberry jam with their bread or biscuits—or even a blackberry pizza for dessert.

A hearty breakfast is a must before a busy day on the ranch. Fancy Egg Scramble with a bowl of just-picked raspberries and fresh blueberry muffins makes a flavorful beginning to the day's activities.

Guests leave the Sonka Sheep Station Inn glowing with the warmth of a beautiful setting, good food, a glimpse of a different lifestyle and the memory of warm hospitality.

Here are some flavorful recipes guests have enjoyed at the inn:

LAMB MARINADE

1-1/2 cups salad oil
3/4 cup soy sauce
1/4 cup Worcestershire sauce
2 tablespoons dry mustard
2-1/4 teaspoons salt
1 tablespoon black pepper
1/2 cup wine vinegar
1-1/2 teaspoons dried parsley
2 crushed garlic cloves
1/3 cup fresh lemon juice

Combine ingredients and mix well. Use for shish kabob, marinating meat cubes in large sealed zip-lock plastic bag overnight. Barbecue or broil lamb kabobs for about 10-15 minutes. Can also be used as a marinade for leg of lamb. **Yield:** 3-1/2 cups marinade.

GREEK GROUND LAMB APPETIZERS

2 pounds lean ground lamb (*or* lamb and beef)
2 eggs, beaten
2/3 cup cracker crumbs
2/3 cup soy sauce
4 tablespoons water
1/8 teaspoon ginger
1/8 teaspoon garlic powder
1/8 teaspoon cumin
1/2 cup pine nuts *or* chopped walnuts

Mix thoroughly and shape into 1-in. balls. Bake on a cookie sheet in a 275° to 300° oven for 35 to 45 minutes. If desired, blend 1/2 cup mustard and 1/2 cup honey as a dip for meatballs. (Or use the Golden Hot Mustard Dip on page 82.) **Yield:** 50 to 60 meatballs.

FANCY EGG SCRAMBLE

1 cup diced Canadian bacon
1/4 cup chopped green onion
3 tablespoons butter
12 eggs, beaten
1 can (3 ounces) mushroom pieces and stems, drained

CHEESE SAUCE
2 tablespoons butter

2 tablespoons flour
1/2 teaspoon salt
1/8 teaspoon pepper
2 cups milk
1 cup grated cheddar cheese

TOPPING
4 tablespoons butter, melted
1/8 teaspoon paprika
2-1/2 cups soft bread crumbs

In large skillet, saute bacon and onion in 3 tablespoons butter until tender but not brown. Add eggs and scramble just until set. Remove from heat; set aside.

To prepare cheese sauce, melt butter; blend in flour, salt and pepper. Add milk gradually. Cook and stir until bubbly. Stir in cheddar cheese until melted. Fold cooked eggs and mushrooms into cheese sauce. Turn into 12- x 7-in. baking dish. Combine topping ingredients and sprinkle over egg mixture. Cover and refrigerate overnight until 30 minutes before baking. Bake uncovered at 350° for 30 minutes. **Yield:** 6 servings.

BAKED ORANGE FRENCH TOAST

1 tablespoon butter
12 slices French bread
8 large eggs
2 cups milk
1/4 cup sugar
1 teaspoon vanilla
1 teaspoon orange extract
1 teaspoon grated orange
1/4 teaspoon salt

Spread butter in a 14-in x 8-in. x 2-in. pan. Arrange bread slices in a single layer. Combine remaining ingredients; beat together and pour over bread. Turn bread to coat evenly. Refrigerate overnight. Place on highest rack and bake at 350° 25-30 minutes until top is light golden brown and puffy. Turn slices over and bake an additional 5-7 minutes. Sprinkle with powdered sugar and serve with favorite syrup. **Yield:** 6 servings.

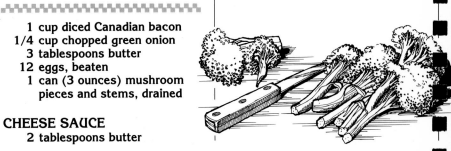

Best Cook

As much as he enjoys cooking, he "enjoys sharing his culinary creations even more," wrote Jean Muncy, as she nominated her husband, Dr. Estle Muncy, Jefferson City, Tennessee, as "Best Cook in the Country".

"Compliments flow freely when he shares his confections, his famous salads, and—most requested of all—his 'Colonel Muncy's Oven-Fried Chicken' (see recipe, page 30)."

Dr. Muncy is a cardiologist and internal medicine specialist in his small, rural community, and he often treats patients and staff to his kitchen creations.

"They know he really cares about them when he shares his tasty, healthful goodies," Jean wrote. "And besides being an excellent cook, he's an accomplished photographer, printer, gardener, catfish farmer and writer... and is active in many civic and professional groups."

IMITATION CRAB/ BROCCOLI CASSEROLE

1 pound fresh broccoli, washed
2 tablespoons margarine
2 tablespoons flour
1 cup skim milk
Dash salt
Dash black pepper
Dash paprika
1/4 cup green onion, thinly sliced
8 ounces imitation crabmeat
1 tablespoon pimiento, coarsely chopped
2 tablespoons slivered almonds

Cut stems of broccoli in bite-size pieces and separate heads into florets. Steam just until bright green in steamer or microwave. Set aside. Make a white sauce by melting margarine in small saucepan, adding onions, then flour and milk. Cook over moderate heat until thickened, stirring constantly. Add salt, pepper and paprika. Fold in crabmeat and pimiento. Arrange broccoli florets around edge of 8-in.-square dish. Fill center with remaining broccoli pieces and spoon crabmeat mixture over broccoli in center of dish. Sprinkle almonds over top. Bake at 375° for 20 minutes or until hot and bubbly. (Casserole can be prepared in advance, refrigerated and heated in microwave, if desired.) **Yield:** 4 servings.

APRICOT CHICKEN ROLLS

1 pound boneless chicken breasts, skin and fat removed
3/4 teaspoon salt
1-1/2 teaspoon instant minced onion
3 tablespoons slivered almonds
About 2/3 cup dried apricots, cut in half
1 tablespoon melted margarine

Lightly pound chicken breasts flat on plastic cutting board. Sprinkle with almonds, apricots and seasonings. Roll each chicken breast into a tight roll; place seam-side down in a baking dish. Brush with margarine; bake at 375° for about 30 minutes. (These can be made with chicken tenders for appetizers. If prepared as appetizers, chop apricots and nuts into smaller pieces.) **Yield:** 4 servings.

BROCCOLI MUSHROOM SALAD

1 pound fresh broccoli
1 large mild onion, Vidalia preferred
1/2 pound fresh mushrooms
Garlic powder
Salt, if desired
1/2 cup lite mayonnaise
1/2 cup plain yogurt
2 tablespoons prepared mustard
1/2 cup cashews

Wash broccoli; cut into bite-size pieces. Chop onion; slice mushrooms thin. Place all vegetables in bowl; sprinkle with garlic powder and salt to taste. Combine mayonnaise, yogurt and mustard; pour over vegetables. Toss gently until all pieces are coated. Cover; refrigerate overnight (or several hours). Stir cashews into mixture just before serving. **Yield:** 10 servings.

WHITE CHOCOLATE CHEX MIX BARS

1 cup Cheerios
1 cup crispix
1 cup fruit loops *or* fruity pebbles
1 cup cocoa krispies *or* cocoa pebbles
1 cup frosted flakes
1 cup Chinese noodles
1-1/2 cups mixed unsalted nuts, chopped
20 ounces white chocolate
2 tablespoons vegetable oil

Combine all cereals, noodles and nuts in large bowl. Pour vegetable oil over white chocolate and microwave on LOW until of stirring consistency. Pour white chocolate mixture over cereal mixture; mix thoroughly using wooden spoon. Press mixture gently into two oiled 13-in. x 9-in. x 2-in. baking pans. Cool to room temperature; cut into squares. **Note:** Any combination of cereals may be substituted for the above. **Yield:** 36 squares.

LOW CHOLESTEROL EGGS: *Separate 3 eggs, reserving whites in small mixing bowl; set aside 1/4 teaspoon egg yolk. Beat whites until fluffy; add 2 tablespoons water and 1 drop yellow food coloring. Beat until smooth. Add measured egg yolk, salt substitute (to taste) and pepper. Cook in non-stick or lightly oiled skillet as scrambled eggs or omelet.* **Diabetic Exchanges:** *One serving equals 1 protein; also, 57 calories, 140 mg sodium, 19 mg cholesterol, 1 gm carbohydrate.*

Big, bountiful, beautiful strawberries! Before you head for the patch to gather yourself a basket, peruse these pick-of-the-crop recipes for some new and wonderful ways to savor summer's berry best.

Make the most of a special occasion with a spectacular chocolate-dipped strawberry pie, or brighten a luncheon with a color-ful, garden-fresh strawberry/rhubarb salad. Tickle your taste buds with a brightly sparkling berry punch.

And when it's time to celebrate the season with family and friends, you'll find new variations for old-fashioned favorites such as home-made strawberry ice cream, sher-bet and shortcake.

SENSATIONAL STRAWBERRIES: Clockwise from lower left—**The Ultimate Strawberry Pie**, Judy Page, Edenville, Michigan (Pg. 43); **Strawberry/Rhubarb Salad**, Joan Truax, Pittsboro, Indiana (Pg. 43); **Strawberry Devonshire Tart**, Carol Ziemann, Chesterfield, Missouri (Pg. 43); **Miniature Strawberry Muffins**, Lois Black, San Antonio, Texas (Pg. 44); **Strawberry Sparkle Punch**, Ida Wester, Shelbina, Missouri (Pg. 43); **Strawberry/Rhubarb Coffee Cake**, Pat Walter, Pine Island, Minnesota (Pg. 44); **Rich Strawberry Short-cake**, Caryn Wiggins, Columbus, Indiana (Pg. 44); **Strawber-ry Ice Cream**, Jeri Dobrowski, Beach, North Dakota (Pg. 43).

Succulent strawberries—they're the sweetest sign of summer. Start the season in style by serving up the tempting treats pictured below—from satisfying salads to delectable desserts.

THE BERRY BEST. Clockwise from upper left—**Strawberry Cheesecake Trifle**, Diane Evens, George, Washington (Pg. 44); **Pavlova**, Gail Payne, Clive, Alberta (Pg. 45); **Super Easy Strawberry Sherbet**, Jane Kennedy, Mayville, Michigan (Pg. 45); **Strawberry/ Spinach Salad,** Perlene Hoekema, Lynden, Washington (Pg. 44).

Recipes from Deb King, Halifax, Pennsylvania.

meals in MINUTES

WHATEVER makes last-minute meals a rush for you—kids, chores, work, fun—you'll appreciate this hearty, nourishing, ready-in-less-that-30-minutes meal.

This speedy menu is quick and colorful, and lets you substitute, add or omit ingredients, depending on what you have on hand.

Substitute fresh asparagus for broccoli in the stir fry, or add crushed red pepper for a little added zip.

If you don't have fresh pineapple, substitute a fruit cup dessert of drained and chilled canned pineapple and mandarin oranges, adding bananas, grapes or whatever is in season.

Begin meal preparation by cooking the rice and cutting up the vegetables for the main dish and washing and chilling the fresh greens. This simple salad is a tasty contrast to the many colors and flavors in the stir fry.

CHICKEN/BROCCOLI STIR FRY

3 tablespoons peanut oil OR vegetable oil of choice
1 pound boneless, skinless chicken breast, cut in bite-size pieces
1 small onion, diced
1 cup celery, cut in 1/2-inch bias cuts
1/2 cup green pepper, cut in bite-size pieces
1-1/2 cups fresh broccoli flowerets OR 1 package (10 ounces) frozen broccoli flowerets, thawed
1 cup carrots, thin, bias cuts
1 cup chicken stock OR bouillon
2 tablespoons cornstarch
1/4 cup water
3 tablespoons soy sauce (reduced sodium okay)
1/4 teaspoon crushed red pepper, optional

Heat oil in wok or in large skillet over a medium-high heat. Saute the chicken pieces until lightly browned; push chicken aside and add onion, cooking and stirring until transparent. Add remaining vegetables; cook, stirring constantly, until vegetables turn bright in color, about 2-3 minutes. Add chicken stock/bouillon; cook for 2 minutes more until vegetables are tender/crisp and chicken is cooked through. Combine cornstarch, water, soy sauce (and red pepper, if desired); add to chicken-vegetable mixture and cook until sauce is slightly thickened and clear. Serve on a bed of rice. **Yield:** 4-5 servings.

FRESH GARDEN LETTUCE/SPINACH SALAD

Washed, chilled leaf lettuce or spinach

TOPPINGS:
Crumbled bacon bits, hulled sunflower seeds OR toasted sesame seeds

BASIC OIL/VINEGAR DRESSING:
3 tablespoons vegetable oil
1 tablespoon white vinegar
1/4 teaspoon dried mustard
Pinch of sugar, if desired
Salt to taste
Fresh ground pepper to taste

Place lettuce/spinach in large bowl or on salad plates; top with choice of toppings. Refrigerate. Combine dressing ingredients and shake vigorously. Just before serving, add dressing and toss salad lightly.

FRESH PINEAPPLE WEDGE

1 large ripe pineapple
Strawberry OR fresh mint garnish
Fortune cookies, if desired

Select a ripe pineapple by choosing fruit that is yellowing and has a sweet aroma. Wash under cold running water, including leaves. Place pineapple on secure cutting surface, greens up. With a sharp knife, cut pineapple in half, then in quarters. With a small knife, cut around "meat" of pineapple, then cut in sections. Garnish with fresh berry or mint. **Yield:** 4-6 generous servings.

COOKING FOR ONE? Prepare a well-balanced meal for four, then use Seal-A-Meal bags or freezer containers to package remaining food in one-serving portions. Next time you don't feel like cooking, pop a frozen meal in the microwave.

MICROWAVE TIP: For best results when reheating food in microwave, always use less than FULL power. Cover with a paper plate or waxed paper.

Recipes and relatives form a flavorful mix at a family reunion picnic—and we've gathered a porchful of recipes that are sure to please!

Two traditional favorites—baked ham and grilled sirloin—are sauced with subtle new tastes, while the perennial potato salad and calico baked beans taste "just like Grandma used to make".

Marinated salads with oil-and-vinegar dressings stand up well in warm weather and can be served as appetizers or a picnic meal-in-a-bowl. Complete the repast with perfect buttermilk yeast buns that make a marvelous complement to meat and are also great to eat simply buttered.

FAMILY REUNION FEAST. Clockwise from lower left—**Old Fashioned Potato Salad**, Margaret Barrow, North Ogden, Utah (Pg. 46); **Raspberry Wine Glazed Ham**, Ruby Nelson, Mountain Home, Arkansas (Pg. 46); **Antipasto Salad**, Marcy Schewe, Danube, Minnesota (Pg. 46); **Marinated Carrot/ Mushroom Salad**, Pat Habiger, Spearville, Kansas (Pg. 47); **Broccoli/ Cauliflower Salad**, Shirley Spade, Nashua, New Hampshire (Pg. 46) **Buttermilk Yeast Buns**, Edna Krahenbuhl, Barron, Wisconsin (Pg. 47); **Three Bean Casserole**, Ida Mae Frey, Topeka, Indiana (Pg. 46); **Onion Buttered Grilled Sirloin**, Margaret Barrow, North Ogden, Utah (Pg. 46).

Sweet treats make picnics perfect, especially after an impromptu softball game, leisurely round of croquet or an afternoon spent pitching horseshoes. Not just any sweets are suited, though—the best bets are desserts that debuted in picnics past.

Help yourself to such savory memories as homemade ice cream, butter pound cakes or rich and portable chocolate treats...desserts that bring back the old-time taste of summer.

SUMMER SWEETS. Clockwise from lower left—**Peanut Butter Candy Cake**, Geraldine Grisdale, Mt. Pleasant, Michigan (Pg. 47); **Orange/Lemon Pound Cake**, Norma Poole, Auburndale, Florida (Pg. 48); **Orange/Pineapple Ice Cream**, Vera Straus, Weidman, Michigan (Pg. 48); **Chewy Chocolate Cookies**, Rosemary Smith, Fort Bragg, California (Pg. 4).

STRAWBERRY/ RHUBARB SALAD
Joan Truax, Pittsboro, Indiana

(PICTURED ON PAGE 36)

4 cups diced raw rhubarb
1-1/2 cups water
1/2 cup sugar
2 packages (3 ounces *each*) strawberry gelatin
1 cup orange juice
1 tablespoon grated orange rind
2 cups fresh strawberries, sliced
Strawberries for garnish

Combine rhubarb, water and sugar in saucepan; cook until tender. Pour hot rhubarb mixture over gelatin and stir until completely dissolved. Add orange juice and rind. Chill until syrupy; fold in strawberries. Pour into a 1-qt. mold; chill until set. Garnish with whole strawberries with hulls. **Yield: 8 servings. Diabetic Exchanges:** One serving equals 3 fruit; also, 167 calories, 69 mg sodium, 0 cholesterol, 41 gm carbohydrate, 3 gm protein, .3 gm fat.

STRAWBERRY DEVONSHIRE TART
Carol Ziemann, Chesterfield, Missouri

(PICTURED ON PAGE 36)

TART SHELL:
1 cup flour
2 tablespoons sugar
1/4 teaspoon salt
6 tablespoons butter, room temperature
1 egg yolk
2 tablespoons ice water

FILLING:
2 packages (3 ounces *each*) cream cheese, softened
1/3 cup dairy sour cream OR yogurt
2 tablespoons sugar
1 quart fresh strawberries, washed, dried & hulled

GLAZE:
1 package (10 ounces) frozen raspberries in syrup, thawed
Water
1/4 cup sugar
1 tablespoon cornstarch

Combine flour, sugar and salt; cut in butter until crumbly. Combine egg yolk and water; stir into flour until dough forms a ball. Press dough onto bottom and up sides of 9-in. tart pan. Prick bottom and sides to prevent excess shrinkage. Bake at 400° for 12-15 minutes until light brown. Cool; set aside. Beat cream cheese until fluffy; beat in sour cream/yogurt and sugar. Spread over bottom of cooled shell. Arrange strawberries, tips up, over cheese. Puree raspberries in blender or processor; pour through sieve to remove seeds. Combine puree with enough water to make 1 cup liquid. In small saucepan, combine sugar and cornstarch. Gradually stir in puree; cook until thick and clear. Cool slightly; pour over strawberries. Chill at least an hour. **Yield: 6-8 servings.**

STRAWBERRY ICE CREAM
Jeri Dobrowski, Beach, North Dakota

(PICTURED ON PAGE 36)

CUSTARD BASE:
4 tablespoons flour
1 cup sugar
1/4 teaspoon salt
2-1/2 cups milk
3 eggs, beaten

1 pint fresh hulled strawberries OR 1-1/2 cups frozen berries, thawed
1 teaspoon lemon juice
1/2 cup sugar

1 cup milk
1 cup heavy cream
1 to 2 tablespoons vanilla

In large glass bowl, blend custard ingredients with a wire whisk. Cook in microwave (or in heavy, 2-qt. saucepan on stove) until mixture coats spoon. Cover with plastic wrap; cool for 2 hours in refrigerator. Mash strawberries, lemon juice and sugar in large bowl or in food processor bowl. (*Don't* add whole berries—they will freeze and be impossible to eat.) Allow fruit to stand about an hour or until juicy. Add strawberries, milk, cream and vanilla to chilled custard mixture; pour into 2-qt. ice cream maker. Follow the manufacturer's instructions for freezing. **Yield: 2 qt.** *or* 10-12 hearty servings.

THE ULTIMATE STRAWBERRY PIE
Judy Page, Edenville, Michigan

(PICTURED ON PAGE 36)

PAT-IN-PAN PIE CRUST:
1-1/2 cups flour
1/2 teaspoon salt
2 tablespoons sugar
1/2 cup vegetable oil
2 tablespoons *cold* milk

FILLING:
11 ounces cream cheese (one 8-ounce + one 3-ounce package), room temperature
4 tablespoons sugar
1 quart fresh strawberries, *divided*
2 ounces semisweet chocolate, melted
1 tablespoon *finely chopped* pistachios, pecans or walnuts

Combine all crust ingredients in 9-in. pie plate; mix and press onto bottom and sides of plate. *Do not prick.* Bake at 400° for 12-15 minutes until golden-brown. Cool. Beat together cream cheese and sugar with mixer until smooth. Add about 3/4 cup of the strawberries; beat until just bits of berry remain. Spread mixture into cooled pie shell. Melt chocolate over low heat; dip tips of remaining strawberries into chocolate. Arrange, tips up, over cream cheese layer. Sprinkle with nuts for garnish. Chill thoroughly. Cut with *sharp* knife. **Yield: 8 servings.**

STRAWBERRY/ SPARKLE PUNCH
Ida Wester, Shelbina, Missouri

(PICTURED ON PAGE 37)

4 cups fresh unsweetened strawberries
1 package (3 ounces) strawberry-flavored gelatin
1 cup boiling water
1 can (6 ounces) frozen lemonade concentrate
1 bottle (32 ounces) cranberry juice cocktail, chilled
2 cups *cold* water
1 bottle (28 ounces) ginger ale, chilled
Strawberries for garnish, if desired

Puree strawberries in blender; place puree in large punch bowl. (Strain; if desired, to remove seeds.) Dissolve gelatin in boiling water; stir in lemonade concentrate. Add mixture to punch bowl. Add cranberry cocktail and *cold* water. Slowly add ginger ale. If desired, serve with fresh strawberry garnish or an ice ring with whole berries frozen in it. **Yield: 28 (4-oz.) servings. Diabetic Exchanges:** One serving equals 1 fruit; also, 65 calories, 10 mg sodium, 17 gm carbohydrate, .5 gm protein, .1 gm fat.

RICH STRAWBERRY SHORTCAKE
Caryn Wiggins, Columbus, Indiana

(PICTURED ON PAGE 37)
2 cups flour
2 tablespoons sugar
4 teaspoons baking powder
1/2 teaspoon salt
1/2 cup butter, softened
1 egg, beaten
About 1/2 cup light cream OR milk
  (half-and-half preferred)

Soft butter
4 cups sweetened, sliced
  strawberries
Whipped cream OR ice cream

Sift together flour, sugar, baking powder and salt. Cut in butter until coarse and crumbly. Combine egg and cream/milk; add to flour mixture, stirring just until dough follows fork around bowl. On lightly floured surface, pat or roll to 1/2-in. thickness. (You may need to work in a little additional flour if the dough is too sticky.) Cut with a 2-1/2-in. round cutter. Bake on ungreased baking sheet in very hot oven, 450° for 8-10 minutes or until biscuits are done. Split biscuits and spread each half with butter. Spoon berries between halves and over top. Serve warm with whipped cream or ice cream. **Yield:** 8 servings.

MINIATURE STRAWBERRY MUFFINS
Lois Black, San Antonio, Texas

(PICTURED ON PAGE 37)
1-1/2 cups *mashed* strawberries
3/4 cup sugar *divided*
1-3/4 cups flour
1/4 teaspoon nutmeg
1/4 teaspoon salt
1/2 teaspoon baking soda
2 eggs, beaten
1/4 cup butter
1 teaspoon vanilla

Combine strawberries and *1/4 cup* sugar; set aside. After 30 minutes, drain strawberries; reserve liquid. Combine flour, nutmeg, salt and soda; set aside. In a medium bowl, mix eggs, butter, vanilla, remaining 1/2 cup sugar and reserved juice from berries. Add to flour mixture; stir until combined. Fold in berries. Spoon into greased miniature muffin tins. Bake at 425° for about 15 minutes for mini muffins, 20 minutes if baking larger muffins. **Yield:** About 32 mini muffins OR 12 large muffins. **Diabetic Exchanges:** One serving (mini) muffin equals 1/2 bread, 1/2 fruit; also 65 calories, 51 mg sodium, 25 mg cholesterol, 11 gm carbohydrate, 1 gm protein, 2 gm fat. One serving (large) muffin equals 1 bread, 1 fruit, 1 fat; also, 174 calories, 136 mg sodium, 67 mg cholesterol, 29 gm carbohydrate, 3 gm protein, 5 gm fat.

STRAWBERRY/RHUBARB COFFEE CAKE
Pat Walter, Pine Island, Minnesota

(PICTURED ON PAGE 37)
FILLING:
4-1/2 cups rhubarb, chopped
24 ounces frozen sliced
  strawberries, thawed
3 tablespoons lemon juice
1-1/2 cups sugar
1/2 cup cornstarch

CAKE:
3 cups flour
1 cup sugar
1 teaspoon baking powder
1 teaspoon salt
1 cup butter, softened
1 cup buttermilk
2 eggs, slightly beaten
1 teaspoon vanilla

TOPPING:
3/4 cup sugar
1/2 cup flour
1/4 cup soft butter

To make filling, combine fruits in saucepan and cook, covered, over medium heat for 5 minutes, stirring occasionally. Add lemon juice, sugar and cornstarch. Cook, stirring, for 5 minutes or until thickened. Cool. To make cake, combine flour, sugar, baking powder and salt in large bowl; cut in butter until mixture is crumbly. Beat together buttermilk, eggs and vanilla; add to the flour mixture. Spread *one-half* of batter in greased 13-in. x 9-in. x 2-in. baking pan. Spread fruit over batter. Spoon remaining batter in small mounds on top of filling. Mix topping ingredients until crumbly; sprinkle over all. Bake at 375° for 45 minutes. Serve slightly warm. **Yield:** 12-16 servings.

STRAWBERRY CHEESECAKE TRIFLE
Diane Evens, George, Washington

(PICTURED ON PAGE 38)
2 packages (8 ounces *each*)
  cream cheese
2 cups confectioners' sugar
1 cup dairy sour cream
1/4 teaspoon *powdered* vanilla OR
  1/2 teaspoon vanilla extract
1/4 teaspoon almond extract
1/2 pint whipping cream
1/2 teaspoon *powdered* vanilla
  OR 1 teaspoon vanilla extract
1 tablespoon sugar
1 angel food cake, torn into
  bite-size pieces
2 quarts fresh strawberries,
  thinly sliced
3 tablespoons sugar
3 tablespoons almond-flavored
  liqueur OR almond extract
  to taste

In a large bowl, cream together cream cheese and sugar; add sour cream, vanilla and almond extract. Set aside. In a small, deep bowl, whip the cream, vanilla and sugar. Fold whipped cream into cream cheese mixture. Add cake pieces; set aside. Combine strawberries, sugar and almond liqueur/extract. Layer together in large glass bowl, starting with strawberries, then adding cake mixture. Continue layering; finish with strawberries. Cover with plastic wrap; chill well. **Yield:** 24 servings.

STRAWBERRY/ SPINACH SALAD
Perlene Hoekema, Lynden, Washington

(PICTURED ON PAGE 38)
2 tablespoons sesame seeds
1-1/2 pounds fresh spinach
1/3 cup vegetable oil
1/3 cup red wine vinegar
1 tablespoon sugar
2 teaspoons minced green
  onion
1/2 teaspoon paprika
1/4 teaspoon Worcestershire
  sauce
2 cups fresh strawberries,
  washed, hulled & halved

In a 7-in. skillet over medium heat, stir sesame seeds until golden; set aside. Wash spinach thoroughly; dry on paper towels and tear into bite-size pieces. Wrap and chill. Blend oil, vinegar, sugar, onion, paprika and

Worcestershire sauce. In large glass bowl, mix together spinach, strawberries, dressing and seeds. **Yield:** 8 servings. **Diabetic Exchanges:** One serving equals 1-1/2 vegetable, 2 fat; also 133 calories, 66 mg sodium, 0 cholesterol, 9 gm carbohydrate, 4 gm protein, 11 gm fat.

SUPER EASY STRAWBERRY SHERBERT

Jane Kennedy, Mayville, Michigan

(PICTURED ON PAGE 38)

2 cups buttermilk
1-1/2 cups strawberry freezer jam*
Fresh strawberries for garnish
Fresh mint leaves for garnish

Stir buttermilk into jam; pour into refrigerator tray and freeze until firm. Cut up frozen mixture; place in chilled mixer bowl. Whip until fluffy. Return to tray; cover and freeze until firm. (Can also freeze in ice cream freezer according to manufacturer's instructions.) Spoon into sherbet dishes. Garnish with fresh strawberries and mint leaves, if desired. **Yield:** About 1 qt.

*STRAWBERRY FREEZER JAM
2 cups fresh mashed strawberries
4 cups granulated sugar
3/4 cup water
1 package (1-3/4 ounces) powdered pectin

Mash strawberries very fine; add sugar; let stand 10 minutes. Place water and pectin in small saucepan; bring to boil. Boil for 1 minute, stirring constantly. Remove from stove; add to strawberries. Stir for 3 minutes. Spoon into clean, sterilized jars, leaving 1/2-in. space at top. Seal; let stand at room temperature for 24 hours. Store jam in freezer. **Yield:** About 5 cups.

♥

PAVLOVA

Gail Payne, Clive, Alberta

(PICTURED ON PAGE 38)
MERINGUE:
4 egg whites, room temperature
1 cup granulated sugar
1 teaspoon cornstarch
1 teaspoon vinegar
1 teaspoon vanilla
CREAM LAYER:
1 cup whipping cream

2 tablespoons granulated sugar
1 teaspoon vanilla
1 pint fresh strawberries
2 kiwi fruits
GLAZE:
1/4 cup granulated sugar
1/4 cup water
1-1/2 teaspoons cornstarch

(**NOTE:** This recipe works best on cool, dry days.)

Beat egg whites until soft peaks form. Gradually add sugar and cornstarch, beating until stiff and glossy. Beat in vinegar and vanilla. (Test meringue by rubbing between thumb and finger—it should not be grainy.) Spread meringue on a foil or parchment paper-lined 12-in. pizza pan (or form in any shape desired). Bake at 275° for 50-60 minutes; turn off heat and allow to stand in oven for at least 1 hour. Make cream layer by whipping cream, sugar and vanilla until stiff. Spread over top of cooled meringue. Arrange fruit in attractive pattern over top of cream layer. Set aside. Combine glaze ingredients in small saucepan. Bring to boil to thicken. Cool. Brush glaze over fruit to seal with small, soft brush. Chill until serving time. **Yield:** 12-16 servings.

STRAWBERRY SAUCE SUPREME

Helen Regan, Carle Place, New York

1-1/2 quarts strawberries, sliced
1/3 cup sugar
1 package (10 ounces) frozen raspberries, thawed
2 tablespoons sugar
2 tablespoons orange liqueur OR 2 teaspoons grated orange rind
1 teaspoon fresh lemon juice

Combine strawberries and sugar; stir to blend. Add raspberries, sugar, liqueur/rind and lemon juice. Refrigerate at least 4 hours. Serve over ice cream, pound cake or angel food cake. **Yield:** About 2 qt.

FRESH STRAWBERRY POUND CAKE

Frances Amundson, Gilby, North Dakota

CAKE:
1 box white cake mix
1 cup crushed fresh strawberries
1 package (3 ounces) strawberry-flavored gelatin

1/2 cup vegetable oil
4 eggs, room temperature
GLAZE:
1/4 cup butter OR margarine
3-1/2 cups confectioners' sugar
1/4 cup mashed strawberries

Combine cake ingredients together in large mixing bowl; mix for 3 minutes. Pour in well-greased-and-floured tube pan. Bake at 325° for 45-55 minutes or until cake tests done. Cool in pan on rack for 10 minutes; remove to serving plate. Combine glaze ingredients until smooth and spread over cake. (May be frozen with or without glaze.)

STRAWBERRIES AND ALMOND CREME

Gail Yeskis, Bridgewater, New Hampshire

1 quart large strawberries
1 package (3-1/2 ounces) vanilla *instant* pudding & pie filling
3/4 cup milk
1 cup heavy *whipped* cream OR nondairy whipped topping
1 to 2 teaspoons almond extract

Carefully wash berries; drain on paper towels. Cut a deep "X" from pointed end of each berry to 1/4 in. from stem end. Gently spread apart to make "petals". Set aside on pretty serving plate. Prepare pudding according to package instructions *except use only 3/4 cup of milk*. Gently fold whipped cream/topping and extract into pudding. Pipe cream into strawberries from a decorating bag with large tip. Serve immediately. **Yield:** 8 servings.

BERRY NICE: Refrigerate fresh strawberries in shallow containers as soon as you pick them, and wash berries in cold water only when you are ready to use them. Do not allow berries to soak.

THE BERRY BEST: Garnish each piece of fresh strawberry pie with a dollop of whipped cream, a mint leaf and one perfect strawberry. • Dip fresh strawberries into sour cream or yogurt and roll in strawberry-flavored gelatin granules for a tasty treat. • Stir homemade strawberry jams and jellies occasionally while they cool to prevent berries from floating to the top. • Strawberries stored with stems stay firm longer than those without stems.

RASPBERRY WINE GLAZED HAM

Ruby Nelson, Mountain Home, Arkansas

(PICTURED ON PAGE 40)

1 (8-10 pound) boneless, fully cooked ham

GLAZE:
* *1/4 cup dry white wine
2 tablespoons lemon juice
2 teaspoons cornstarch
1/3 cup seedless raspberry jam, divided
1 tablespoon butter
Watercress *or* parsley

Score ham in diamond shapes; place on a rack in shallow roasting pan. Bake at 325° about 2 hours until meat thermometer registers 140°. (Ham may also be done on a gas grill or charcoal barbecue—follow manufacturer's directions.) In a saucepan, blend wine and lemon juice into cornstarch. Add about 1/2 of jam. Cook and stir until thickened and bubbly. Stir in remaining jam and butter. Heat and stir until butter is melted. Brush ham with glaze. Bake ham 10 minutes more. Spoon any additional glaze over ham. *You may want to double the glaze recipe and thin it slightly with water to pass with ham. Garnish ham with watercress or parsley.

ANTIPASTO SALAD

Marcy Schewe, Danube, Minnesota

(PICTURED ON PAGE 40)

2 green peppers
3 tomatoes
1/4 pound provolone cheese
1/4 pound hard salami, Genoa preferred, sliced thin, quartered
1/4 pound pepperoni, sliced thin
1 small onion, minced

EASY EGGS: To cook eggs for potato salad, break them into bowl and prick yolks with toothpick. Cover; microwave on MEDIUM-HIGH (1 minute per egg). Cool, cut for salad.

SAFER SALADS: Keep all perishable picnic foods in a well-insulated cooler with plenty of ice. Keep the cooler closed and in a shady spot.

2 stalks celery, cut in thin, bias cuts
1 can (6 ounces) pitted black olives, drained
1 jar (5 ounces) stuffed green olives, drained
About 1 pound rotini *or* shell pasta, cooked, drained and cooled

DRESSING:
2/3 cup olive *or* vegetable oil
1/2 cup red wine vinegar
1 teaspoon leaf oregano, crumbled
1 teaspoon pepper
Salt to taste, if desired

Cut peppers, tomatoes and cheese into bite-sized chunks in large mixing bowl. Add salami, pepperoni, onion, olives and pasta; stir to blend. Combine dressing ingredients; shake well to blend. Pour over salad ingredients; stir to blend. Refrigerate, covered, overnight. **Yield:** 15-20 servings.

OLD FASHIONED POTATO SALAD

Margaret Barrow, North Ogden, Utah

(PICTURED ON PAGE 40)

5 medium potatoes cooked, jackets slipped and slightly cooled (about 6 cups diced)
1-1/4 teaspoons salt
1/4 teaspoon pepper

SALAD DRESSING:
3/4 cup salad dressing
3/4 cup mayonnaise
1 teaspoon sugar
2 tablespoons dill pickle juice
1 tablespoon vinegar
1 tablespoon sweet pickle juice
1/4 teaspoon celery salt
Dash onion salt
5 green onions, thinly sliced
2 tablespoons diced sweet pickle
6 hard cooked eggs, peeled and diced

GARNISH:
Hard cooked eggs, peeled and sliced
Green pepper rings
Paprika

Combine diced potatoes, salt and pepper in large bowl. Combine dressing ingredients and pour over still warm potatoes, mixing thoroughly. Let stand in refrigerator for at least 2 hours; overnight is preferred. Add green onions, sweet pickle and diced eggs; mix thoroughly. Garnish with additional eggs, pepper rings and paprika, if desired. Serve chilled. **Yield:** 8 servings.

THREE BEAN CASSEROLE

Ida Mae Frey, Topeka, Indiana

(PICTURED ON PAGE 41)

8 strips bacon
2 large onions, cut into rings
1-1/2 teaspoons garlic powder
1 teaspoon dry mustard
1/2 cup brown sugar
1/4 cup cider vinegar
1 can (16 ounces) dark red kidney beans, drained
1 can (16 ounces) New England baked beans, undrained
1 can (16 ounces) green lima beans, drained

Fry bacon until crisp; drain on paper towels, crumble and set aside. Place onion rings, garlic powder, mustard, brown sugar and vinegar in large skillet. Cover; cook 20 minutes over medium heat. Combine beans in 3 quart casserole. Stir in bacon and onion mixture, blending ingredients. Bake, covered, at 350° for 45 minutes. **Yield:** 10 servings.

BROCCOLI/ CAULIFLOWER SALAD

Shirley Spade, Nashua, New Hampshire

(PICTURED ON PAGE 41)

1 bunch broccoli, small flowerettes *only*
1 head cauliflower, broken into small flowerettes
1 can (6 ounces) pitted ripe olives, drained
1 jar (6 ounces) stuffed green olives, drained
8 ounces feta cheese, crumbled
1 pint tiny cherry tomatoes, whole
1 cup Italian salad dressing

Place all ingredients in large bowl, preferably one with seal-on lid. Toss to coat. Marinate in refrigerator at least 8 hours, tossing occasionally to distribute marinade over vegetables. **Yield:** 3-4 quarts.

ONION BUTTERED GRILLED SIRLOIN

Margaret Barrow, North Ogden, Utah

(PICTURED ON PAGE 41)

STEAK SAUCE:
1/2 cup butter
1/4 cup fresh minced parsley
1/4 cup minced onion

2 teaspoons Worcestershire
  sauce
1/2 teaspoon dry mustard
1/2 teaspoon black pepper
  3 to 4 pounds sirloin steak,
  1-1/2-inch-thick cut

Combine sauce ingredients in saucepan and heat (or microwave in glass container) until butter melts. Set aside. Slash edges of beef sirloin steak. Broil 3-4 inches from heat for 10-12 minutes on each side (rare) or 14-16 minutes (for medium) brushing frequently with butter mixture. Steak may also be grilled on gas or charcoal barbecue following manufacturer's instructions. **Yield:** 6-8 servings.

> **BETTER BREAD:** To freshen day-old or slightly dry rolls or bread, microwave on paper towel on DE-FROST/LOW (8 ounces heats in 1-1/4 minutes).

BUTTERMILK
YEAST BUNS
Edna Krahenbuhl, Barron, Wisconsin

(PICTURED ON PAGE 41)
1/2 cake (1 ounce) compressed
  yeast *or* 1 package active dry
  yeast
1/4 cup warm water (110-115°)
  3 cups buttermilk, room
  temperature
1/2 cup sugar
1/2 cup butter, melted
  2 eggs, beaten
  1 teaspoon baking soda
  1 teaspoon salt
About 8 cups all purpose flour

Crumble yeast into warm water in large mixing bowl; stir to dissolve. Add buttermilk and sugar; let mixture stand 15 minutes. Add *warm* butter and eggs; mix. Sift soda and salt with 4 cups flour; add to liquid mixture. Beat until smooth batter forms. Add remaining sifted flour, stirring with spoon until dough is no longer sticky. Knead on floured board; place in large greased mixing bowl. Cover; let rise until double, about 1 hour. Punch dough down; form into buns (squeeze dough into balls the size of egg). Place on greased baking sheet; flatten slightly with hand. Let rise until double, about 30 minutes. Bake at 400° for 15-20 minutes or until light golden brown. Remove to cooling rack; brush tops with melted butter. **Yield:** About 4 dozen buns.

MARINATED CARROT/
MUSHROOM SALAD
Pat Habiger, Spearville, Kansas

(PICTURED ON PAGE 41)
DRESSING:
2/3 cup vinegar
2/3 cup vegetable oil
1/4 cup chopped onion
  2 cloves garlic, minced
  1 teaspoon salt *or* to taste
1/4 teaspoon fresh ground pepper
  1 teaspoon sugar
  1 teaspoon leaf basil, crumbled
  1 teaspoon leaf oregano,
  crumbled
  2 cups sliced carrots, cooked
  1 can (14 ounces) artichoke
  hearts, drained and cut in
  quarters
  8 ounces fresh mushrooms,
  halved
  1 cup pitted ripe olives, halved
  1 jar (2 ounces chopped
  pimento) drained *or* 1/4 cup
  chopped red pepper

In saucepan, combine dressing ingredients; bring to a boil. Reduce heat; simmer, uncovered, for 10 minutes. Combine carrots, artichoke hearts, mushrooms, olives and pimento/pepper in large bowl. Pour hot dressing over vegetables, stirring to coat. Cover; chill for several hours, stirring occasionally. Drain; serve in lettuce-lined bowl. **Yield:** 2 quarts.

PEANUT BUTTER
CANDY CAKE
Geraldine Grisdale, Mt. Pleasant, Michigan

(PICTURED ON PAGE 42)
CAKE:
1-3/4 cups boiling water
  1 cup quick-cooking rolled oats
1/2 cup butter *or* margarine
  1 cup *light* brown sugar
  1 cup white sugar
  1 teaspoon vanilla
  2 eggs
1-1/2 cups unsifted all purpose flour
  1 teaspoon baking soda
1/2 teaspoon baking powder
1/4 teaspoon cinnamon
1/4 teaspoon salt
  5 (.6 ounce size) milk chocolate
covered peanut butter cups

FROSTING:
  3 tablespoons butter
  3 ounces unsweetened
  chocolate
About 3 cups confectioners' sugar
1/4 teaspoon salt

1/2 cup milk
  1 teaspoon vanilla

Combine water and rolled oats; cool to room temperature. Set aside. Cream together butter, brown sugar, sugar and vanilla; beat in eggs. Blend in oatmeal mixture. Combine flour, baking soda, baking powder, cinnamon and salt; add to creamed mixture. Beat 1 minute on medium speed. Pour batter into greased and floured 13-inch x 9-inch x 2-inch pan. Chop peanut butter cups and sprinkle on top of batter (*do not stir*). Bake at 350° for 40-45 minutes or until cake tests done. For frosting, melt butter in small saucepan. Add chocolate; stir constantly over *very* low heat until melted. Pour into small mixing bowl. Add remaining ingredients; beat until well blended. Chill to spreading consistency, 10-15 minutes. Frost cake. **Yield:** 16-20 servings.

CHEWY CHOCOLATE
COOKIES
Rosemary Smith, Fort Bragg, California

(PICTURED ON PAGE 42)
1-1/4 cups butter *or* margarine,
  softened
1-3/4 to 2 cups sugar
  2 eggs
  2 teaspoons vanilla
  2 cups all purpose flour
3/4 cup unsweetened cocoa
  1 teaspoon baking soda
Dash salt
  1 cup chopped nuts, optional

Cream butter *or* margarine and sugar in large bowl. Add eggs and vanilla; blend well. Combine flour, cocoa, soda and salt; gradually blend into creamed mixture Stir in nuts, if desired. Drop by teaspoonfuls onto ungreased cookie sheet. Bake at 350° for 8-9 minutes. *Do not overbake.* Cookies will be soft. Cool on sheets until set, about 1 minute. Remove to wire rack to cool completely. Store in airtight container. **Yield:** About 4-1/2 dozen.

> **CHILLING BEVERAGES:** To chill soda and other beverages for a large party, put bottles and cans in your washing machine, then cover with ice and cold water. When the party's over, spin out the water ...no mess to clean!

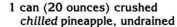

ORANGE/LEMON POUND CAKE
Norma Poole, Auburndale, Florida

(PICTURED ON PAGE 42)

POUND CAKE:
    1 cup butter, softened
    1/4 cup vegetable shortening
    2 cups sugar
    5 eggs, room temperature
    3 cups all purpose flour
    1/2 teaspoon salt
    1/2 teaspoon baking soda
    1/2 teaspoon baking powder
    1 cup buttermilk, room
      temperature
    1 teaspoon vanilla extract
    1 teaspoon lemon extract

GLAZE:
    2 teaspoons grated orange rind
    2 teaspoons grated lemon rind
    2 tablespoons orange juice,
      fresh preferred
    2 tablespoons lemon juice,
      fresh preferred
    1 cup confectioners' sugar

Cream together butter, shortening and sugar until light and fluffy. Add eggs, one at a time, beating well after each addition. Combine flour, salt, soda and baking powder to creamed mixture alternately with buttermilk, ending with dry ingredients. Beat well after each addition. Add extracts. Spoon batter into well-greased and floured 10-inch tube or bundt pan. Bake at 325° for 45-60 minutes or until cake tests done when a wooden pick inserted in center comes out dry and clean. Meanwhile, make glaze by combining all ingredients, blending well. Set aside. Cool cake in pan on wire rack for 15 minutes; remove from pan. Place cake on wire rack over plate that is slightly larger. Punch holes in still-warm cake with wooden pick and drizzle glaze over cake repeatedly until absorbed. **Yield:** 12-16 servings.

ORANGE/PINEAPPLE ICE CREAM
Vera Straus, Weidman, Michigan

(PICTURED ON PAGE 42)
    1 package (6 ounces) orange-
      pineapple gelatin
    2 cups boiling water
    4 eggs
1-1/2 cups sugar
    2 tablespoons flour
    1/4 teaspoon salt
    2 cups half-and-half

    1 can (20 ounces) crushed
      chilled pineapple, undrained
    1 can (14 ounces) sweetened
      condensed milk, chilled
    1 carton (8 ounces) nondairy
      frozen whipped topping,
      thawed
    1 can (12 ounces) frozen
      orange-pineapple concentrate,
      thawed, *undiluted*

Dissolve gelatin in boiling water; let cool to room temperature. Set aside. Beat eggs in large bowl on medium speed of electric mixer until frothy. Add sugar, flour, salt and half-and-half, mixing to blend. Place mixture in heavy saucepan over medium heat, stirring constantly until mixture coats back of a spoon (soft custard), about 10 minutes. (Mixture may also be cooked in a microwave.) Cool; stir in gelatin mixture and pineapple, condensed milk, whipped topping and concentrate. Chill ingredients thoroughly (overnight is best). Pour into freezer can of a 1-gallon ice cream maker. Freeze according to manufacturer's directions. Allow ice cream flavors to ripen at least 1 hour before serving. **Yield:** 1 gallon.

ITALIAN CREAM CAKE
Floyce Day, Broxton, Georgia

    5 eggs, separated
    1/2 cup (1 stick) butter or
      margarine
    1/2 cup shortening
    2 cups sugar
    2 cups flour
    1 teaspoon baking soda
Pinch salt
    1 cup buttermilk
    1 teaspoon vanilla
    1 small can flaked coconut
    1 cup nuts, chopped

FROSTING:
    1/4 cup butter or margarine
    8 ounces cream cheese
    1 teaspoon vanilla
    4 cups confectioners' sugar
Milk to mix
Chopped nuts (sprinkle on frosting

between layers on top of cake)

Beat egg whites until stiff; set aside. Cream butter, shortening and sugar. Add egg yolks. Mix well. Sift together flour, soda and salt. Add to creamed mixture alternately with buttermilk. Add vanilla, coconut and nuts. Fold in stiffly beaten egg whites. Pour into four layer pans. Bake at 350° for 20-25 minutes until cake springs back to touch. Beat together all frosting ingredients except nuts. Frost, sprinkling nuts on frosting between layers.

FRESH STRAWBERRIES AND CREME
Gayle Wilson, Cedarville, Illinois

CREME:
    1 package (8 ounces) cream
      cheese, softened
    1 cup dairy sour cream
    1/3 cup confectioners' sugar
    2 teaspoons orange liqueur OR
    1/4 teaspoon grated
      orange rind
Miniature chocolate cups OR mini
  biscuit cases
    2 quarts fresh strawberries

Combine creme ingredients in small mixing bowl; beat until smooth. Chill an hour or overnight to blend flavors. To serve, place chocolate cups or mini biscuit cases on pretty plate; fill one-half full with creme mixture. Top with one whole, washed strawberry. To eat, dip berry in creme. **Yield:** 8 servings.

GERMAN CHOCOLATE ICE CREAM
Cynthia Kolberg Syracuse, Indiana

    1 cup sugar
    1/4 cup flour
    1/4 teaspoon salt
    1/4 teaspoon cinnamon
    1 quart milk
    2 bars (4 ounces *each*) German
      sweet chocolate, melted
    3 eggs, beaten
    1 cup shredded coconut
    1 quart light cream or
      half-and-half
    1 cup chopped pecans

Combine sugar, flour, salt and cinnamon in heavy 3-quart saucepan. Gradually add milk. Cook over medium heat, stirring constantly until thickened. Cook 2 more minutes. Remove from heat. Blend in melted chocolate. Blend small amount of cooked mixture into eggs, stirring constantly. Return mixture to pan. Cook 1 minute. **Do Not Boil.** Remove from heat; add coconut. Blend in cream. Chill mixture 1-2 hours. Stir in nuts just before freezing. Freeze following ice cream maker's instructions. **Yield:** 1 gallon.

CARROT/WALNUT SALAD

Donna Thompson, Sweet Springs, Missouri

- 2 cups finely shredded raw carrots
- 1/2 cup walnuts, coarsely chopped
- 1/2 cup raisins
- 1/2 cup coconut

DRESSING:
- 1 egg, beaten
- 1/3 cup sugar
- 3 tablespoons light cream, half-and-half or evaporated milk
- 2 tablespoons vinegar
- 1/4 teaspoon salt

Shred carrots with fine shredder in food processor or grind (as Donna does) with a hand-turned food grinder. Add walnuts, raisins and coconut. Set aside. Combine in heavy small saucepan, beaten egg, sugar, cream, vinegar and salt. Cook, stirring constantly over medium heat. Cool to room temperature. Pour over carrot mixture; stir to blend. Let stand, covered, in refrigerator for 2-3 hours. **Yield:** 6-8 servings.

CALIFORNIA CLUB SALAD

Alex Michaels, Claremont, California

- 4 stalks celery, washed and drained
- 2 chicken breasts, skinned, boned, cooked and cooled
- 4 ounces Monterey Jack cheese
- 4 medium green onions
- 2 large tomatoes
- 8 ounces lean bacon, cooked until crisp
- 1 cup loose, long-stemmed cilantro
- 2 slices sourdough bread
- 2 tablespoons soft butter
- 4 tablespoons grated Parmesan cheese

DRESSING:
- 1-1/2 tablespoons mayonnaise
- 3 tablespoons dairy sour cream
- 1 teaspoon Dijon mustard
- 1-1/2 tablespoons honey

Leaf lettuce, washed, drained and chilled

Cut celery, chicken, cheese, onions and tomato in short, thin sticks, about 3-in. x 1/8-in. x 1/4-in. julienne cuts. Keep ingredients separate; set aside. Cut cilantro in similar lengths. Toast slices of bread in toaster oven or broiler until light golden brown on both sides. Remove and butter one side only. Sprinkle with Parmesan cheese; return to toaster oven or broiler and toast until Parmesan cheese bubbles. Remove; slice in similar sizes to other salad ingredients. Set aside. Cook bacon in microwave until crisp; break into pieces 1/2-inch long; set aside. Combine salad dressing ingredients thoroughly. Right before serving, blend all salad ingredients with dressing. Serve immediately from glass lettuce-lined bowl. **Yield:** 8 servings.

✓ FAVORITE NICOISE SALAD

Mrs. Eddie Paulson, Stanley, North Dakota

- 3 cups boiled potatoes, sliced 1/4 inch thick
- 1 pound *fresh* green beans, cooked, drained
- 1 can (7-ounce) albacore (white) tuna
- 3 ounces olive oil
- 3 ounces vinegar
- 1 teaspoon salt
- 1/4 teaspoon white pepper
- 2 teaspoons Dijon mustard

Romaine lettuce leaves
- 2 tomatoes, quartered
- 12 pitted black olives

Capers (optional)

Gently mix cooked potatoes, green beans and drained tuna in large bowl. Set aside. Make dressing by mixing olive oil, vinegar, salt, pepper and mustard together. Pour over potato mixture; toss lightly. Arrange lettuce on plates; mound with salad. Decorate with tomatoes, olives and capers, if desired. Serve immediately; refrigerate leftovers. **Yield:** 6 servings. **Diabetic Exchanges:** One serving equals 1 protein, 1 bread, 1 vegetable, 2 fats; also 480 mg sodium, 21 mg cholesterol, 261 calories, 20 gm carbohydrate.

SOUR MILK DOUGHNUTS

Ada Urie, Glover, Vermont

- 3-1/2 cups sifted all-purpose flour
- 1 teaspoon baking soda
- 1/4 teaspoon baking powder
- 1 teaspoon salt
- 1 teaspoon nutmeg
- 1/2 teaspoon ginger
- 3/4 cup sugar
- 2 tablespoons lard OR shortening
- 2 eggs
- 1 cup sour milk*

Lard OR vegetable oil for deep frying

*Try to use freshly soured milk that is a thick clabber; otherwise dough will be too soft. Sift flour, baking soda, powder, salt, nutmeg and ginger 3 times. Set aside. Cream sugar and lard well. Add eggs, beating well with electric beater. Add sour milk; beat well. Stir in dry ingredients all at once; stir well. DO NOT BEAT. Chill dough overnight. Divide dough in half; roll out on floured board about 1/4 in. thick. Cut with doughnut cutter. Fry in fresh lard or vegetable oil at 400°. **Yield:** 2 dozen.

SOUR CREAM SCALLOPED POTATOES

Estelle Blasel, Orange, California

- 2 large baking potatoes
- 1 medium-size onion, diced
- 2 tablespoons butter
- 1 cup cultured sour cream
- 4 hard-cooked eggs, sliced

Salt
Ground pepper
Paprika

Pare and slice potatoes 1/8 in. thick. Parcook in boiling, salted water 5 minutes; drain. Set aside. Saute onion in butter until glossy but not brown. Stir in sour cream and let heat thoroughly. DO NOT BOIL. In buttered 2-qt. casserole, layer 1/2 of potatoes, egg slices and sour cream mixture. Sprinkle salt, pepper and paprika lightly over sour cream mixture. Repeat layers with rest of ingredients. Bake, uncovered, at 350° for 45 minutes or until potatoes are tender. Do not overbake. **Yield:** 4 servings.

Country Inns

Asphodel

Route 2, Box 89
Jackson, Louisiana 70748
504/654-6868

Directions: From Baton Rouge, take I-110 north to Hwy. 61 North; 10 miles on 61 to Hwy. 68; right (east) about 8 miles to inn.

Innkeeper: Owen Kemp

Schedule: Open daily except Christmas Day.

Rates and Accommodations: 18 guest rooms with private baths, $40-$70 double occupancy, including full breakfast. Restaurant open daily to inn guests and public for lunch, 11:30 a.m. to 3 p.m.; dinner 5:30 p.m. to 8 p.m. (reservations requested). Seminar facilities available for up to 40 people. Gift shop offers a wide variety of regional gifts and crafts. Visa, Master Card, American Express, personal checks accepted. Hours and rates subject to change. Please call or write.

Authentic Southern-style home cooking is the rule at this old-fashioned plantation inn. The menu at Asphodel changes daily, featuring a fresh fish or seafood, poultry, pork or beef entree each day. The inn is known for its Creole and Cajun foods, such as blackened catfish, dirty rice and jambalaya with chicken and sausage.

And the inn is always happy to make a sack lunch for a relaxing outdoor meal or to take with sightseeing. Imagine opening your miniature shopping bag to find Southern fried chicken, ham and cheese croissants, a crisp apple and a huge homemade chocolate-chip cookie!

The French doors of the dining room open onto a wrap-around veranda, where guests can relax (bar service available) before dinner. Imagine the soft Southern breeze blowing through the room as you savor dishes such as these:

TURKEY INN BETWEEN

SAUCE
- 1/4 pound butter
- 1/2 bunch chopped green onions
- 1/2 cup flour
- 2 cups milk
- 2 cups turkey gravy
- 1 can of mushroom stems and pieces (4 ounces), including liquid
- 8 generous slices of cooked turkey breast
- 8 servings of sliced baked ham
- 3 boxes frozen cut broccoli
- 1/2 cup Gruyere cheese, grated

Melt butter in heavy saucepan. Saute green onions until slightly softened. Add flour, stirring until well blended. Add milk and stir until sauce thickens. Add gravy and mushrooms and heat thoroughly.

For each serving, place a slice of turkey and a slice of ham in a casserole dish. Cover with cooked broccoli. Pour sauce over all and top with grated cheese. Bake at 350° until cheese melts, about 15 minutes. **Yield:** 8 servings.

CURRIED PINEAPPLE CHICKEN SALAD

- 2 frying chickens, 2 to 2-1/2 pounds each
- 1 can drained diced pineapple chunks *or* tidbits
- 1 cup chopped celery
- 2 tablespoons curry powder
- 1/2 cup white raisins
- 1/2 cup chopped green onions, including tops
- 1/2 cup broken pecans
- Mayonnaise to bind
- Salt and pepper

Cook chickens. Discard skin and bones; dice the meat. Mix with remaining ingredients and serve very cold on a bed of lettuce. **Yield:** 8-12 servings.

DIRTY RICE

- 2 to 4 strips of bacon
- 1 cup long grain rice
- 1/2 cup green onions, chopped, including tops
- 1 cup chopped onion
- 6 chicken livers, chopped
- 3 cups water
- 2 cloves garlic, minced
- 1/2 teaspoon dried thyme
- 1/4 cup chopped parsley
- Salt and red pepper to taste

Brown bacon in heavy skillet or Dutch oven; set aside. Over low heat, fry onions in bacon fat until they just turn brown. Add chicken livers and stir until they lose their wet look. Add raw rice, stirring until rice is a nutty brown. Add water, bacon (chopped in half pieces) and seasonings. Simmer until rice is tender. **Yield:** 6 servings.

COUNTRY CAPTAIN CHICKEN

- 2-1/2 to 3-pound frying chicken
- 1 cup flour
- 1 tablespoon bacon fat
- 1/2 cup butter
- 1 large onion, finely chopped
- 2 cloves garlic
- 1/2 cup seedless raisins
- 1 cup water
- 1 tablespoon curry powder
- 1 green pepper, chopped
- 2 large fresh tomatoes *or* 1 cup canned tomatoes
- 1/2 cup pecans, coarsely chopped
- Salt and pepper to taste
- Dash of Tabasco
- 1 tablespoon peach brandy, optional

Cut the chicken into serving pieces. Salt and pepper and dredge in flour. Heat skillet with oil or bacon fat before adding butter (to keep butter from scorching.) Fry chicken just to brown—it need not be fully cooked. Remove chicken from pan. Add onions and stir in butter left in pan until they are soft and transparent. Chop garlic fine or squeeze through press and add with remaining ingredients. When gravy has reached a simmer, return chicken and cook until tender. Serve over rice. **Yield:** 4 to 6 servings.

QUICK BREAD CRUMBS: To make dry bread crumbs, cut six slices of bread into 1/2 inch cubes. Microwave on HIGH in 3-qt. casserole 6-7 minutes, stirring after 3 minutes. Crush in blender.

Best Cook

Garden-fresh ingredients all year long are part of what makes Cathy Ireland, Flint, Michigan, the "Best Cook in the Country", according to her mother, Alice Robinson of Otisville.

"Cathy cooks the most delicious, nutritious meals!" Alice wrote. "She grows a beautiful garden every summer, canning and freezing enough vegetables to last through the year—and gives many to friends, too.

"She has three daughters, but she's mother to every child she meets, including those who ride her school bus. Cathy decorates her bus for holidays, and hands out homemade treats to the children. She's a Girl Scout leader, and teaches her troop to cook interesting, tasty dishes and make new crafts as well. As Summer Day Camp Director in our county, she's loved by all the young people she comes in contact with—they enjoy camp because she has so much love to give.

"Cathy's one of the busiest people I know, yet finds time to be involved with her daughters' many activities," Alice continued. "And it's a treat to be invited to her house for dinner, because I know that the meal will be outstanding. I am very proud of her!"

QUICK TACO PIE

1 pound ground beef
1/2 cup chopped onion
1 package (1-1/4 ounces) taco seasoning mix
3/4 cup biscuit mix
1-1/4 cups milk
3 eggs
1 cup shredded cheddar cheese
1/4 head iceberg lettuce, shredded
1 tomato, diced
1/3 cup sliced ripe olives

Cook and stir ground beef and onion in skillet until beef is brown; drain. Stir in seasoning mix; spoon into greased 8-in. square dish. Set aside. Beat biscuit mix, milk and eggs with wire whisk or hand beater until almost smooth, about 1 minute. Pour over meat. Bake at 400° for 25-30 minutes or until center is set. Sprinkle with cheese; bake 2 minutes more or until cheese is melted. Cool for 5 minutes; garnish with lettuce, tomatoes, olives and, if desired, sour cream. **Yield:** 6-8 servings.

FRIED GRITS AND SAUSAGE (MUSH)

1 pound bulk pork sausage
4 cups water
1 teaspoon salt
1 cup quick-cooking grits
1/2 cup cornmeal
Pepper to taste
4 tablespoons butter or margarine

Cook sausage until brown; drain well. Set aside. Bring water and salt to boil; stir in grits. Return to boiling; reduce heat. Cook 3 minutes, stirring occasionally. Remove from heat. Add sausage, cornmeal and pepper. Stir well; spread in 9-in. x 5-in. bread pan. Refrigerate overnight. Slice 1/2 in. thick and fry in skillet over medium heat in butter or margarine. Serve with syrup or applesauce, if desired. **Yield:** 8 servings.

LAZY DAY LASAGNE

12 ounces lasagne noodles
1/2 teaspoon leaf oregano, crumbled

2 cans (15-1/2 ounces *each*) spaghetti sauce with meat
2 cups cottage cheese
12 ounces sliced mozzarella cheese

Cook noodles following package directions; drain. Stir oregano into sauce. Layer *half of* noodles, cottage cheese, mozzarella cheese and sauce in 13-in. x 9-in. x 2-in. baking pan. Repeat layers. Bake at 350° for about 1 hour or until bubbly. **Yield:** 8 servings.

STRAWBERRY SHORTCUT CAKE

1 cup miniature marshmallows
2 cups (2 packages, 10 ounces each) frozen, sliced strawberries in syrup, *thawed*
1 package (3 ounces) strawberry gelatin dessert
2-1/4 cups flour, unsifted
1-1/2 cups sugar
1/2 cup vegetable shortening
3 teaspoons baking powder
1/2 teaspoon salt
1 cup milk
1 teaspoon vanilla
3 eggs

Grease bottom only of 13-in. x 9-in. x 2-in. baking pan. Sprinkle marshmallows evenly over bottom of pan; set aside. Thoroughly combine thawed strawberries and syrup with gelatin; set aside. In large mixer bowl, combine remaining ingredients. Blend at low speed until moistened; beat 3 minutes at medium speed. Carefully pour batter evenly over marshmallows in pan. Spoon strawberry mixture evenly over batter. Bake at 350° for 45-50 minutes until golden brown and toothpick inserted in center comes out clean. Serve warm or cool with ice cream or whipped cream. **Yield:** 16-20 servings.

SOUR CREAM SECRETS: Always stir in sour cream at the end of cooking. • Never boil sour cream (unless a recipe specifically calls for it.) • Heat sour cream only at low temperatures. • Fold sour cream in gently when adding it to other ingredients. • One tablespoon of sour cream has only 25 calories...compared with 101 in mayonnaise.

R ed, ripe and juicy, tomatoes are tops in taste eaten simply seasoned with the sun's warmth. But the season for garden-fresh tomatoes is much too short.

Recapture that fresh-from-the-vine flavor as you treat family and friends to this colorful collection of top tomato dishes. Pick out a perfect pasta and tomato treat or a tomato and vegetable pizza...savor a satisfying tomato side dish, main dish salad or snappy taco sauce.

Surprise someone with tomatoes "in disguise" in a batch of green tomato mincemeat, fragrant with fruit and spices, or even in a moist chocolate cake!

You can count on compliments when you serve one of these tasty tomato dishes. So make enough for seconds!

RED-LETTER RECIPES! Clockwise from lower left: **Tomatoes Provencale**, Leatrice Simpkins, Cambridge City, Indiana (Pg. 59); **Kansas Taco Sauce**, Nila Miller, Frankfort, Kansas (Pg. 59); **Green Tomato Mincemeat**, Yvette Knight, New Gloucester, Maine (Pg. 59); **Corn and Tomato Casserole**, Edna Hoffman, Hebron, Indiana (Pg. 60); **Green Tomato Chocolate Cake**, Dorothy Kubota, Sacramento, California (Pg. 60); **Sweet Tomato Pie**, Rita Futral, Ocean Springs, Mississippi (Pg. 60); **Hot Chicken, Wild Rice and Tomato Salad**, Jeanette Strobel, Brainerd, Minnesota (Pg. 60); and **Fresh Vegetable Pizza**, Jan Hill, Sacramento, California (Pg. 59).

Taste-tempting tomatoes—summer would not be the same without them! America's No. 1 home garden crop can be served up simply sliced or cleverly cooked in appealing appetizers, marvelous marinated salads and savory soups and sauces such as those pictured below.

TANTALIZING TOMATOES! Clockwise from bottom—**Marinated Herbed Tomato Salad**, Frieda Meding, Trochu, Alberta (Pg. 60); **Appetizer Tomato Cheese Bread**, Penney Kester, Springville, New York (Pg. 61); **Fresh Tomato Soup**, Rosemarie Johnson, Norridge, Illinois (Pg. 61); **Stuffed Cherry Tomatoes**, Donna Smith, Grey Cliff, Montana (Pg. 61).

Recipes from Alice Ellison, Plymouth, Minnesota.

meals in MINUTES

AAH, SUMMERTIME. It's a time for rest and relaxation...for that respite you've been waiting for.

Truth is, you're probably more rushed this time of year than any other, with family fun...yard work...and yes, some leisure time. But this time of year is also when it's easier than ever to make quick meals visually appealing and attractive. Fresh garden produce—whether from your back yard or a stand—does the trick.

Corn on the cob just can't be beat, and you can make the most delicious of desserts from soft summer fruit.

One of the best things about this "Meals in Minutes" menu is that it can be turned out either indoors or out. In good weather, turn to the grill. On rainy days, broil the kabobs in the oven in just minutes.

SUMMER SAUSAGE KABOB

      1 pound sweet Italian link
        sausage, cut in 1-inch pieces
      1 cup water
      6 large mushrooms
      1 tablespoon butter
      1 red and 1 green sweet pepper,
        cut in chunks

Simmer sausage in water for 5-10 minutes; set aside. Simmer mushrooms in butter and enough water to cover for 3-4 minutes to soften. Alternate the sausage, mushrooms and peppers on skewers; grill 7-8 minutes on each side. (Can also be broiled in oven 3-4 in. from heat source for the same time.) **Yield:** 2-3 servings.

CORN ON THE COB

As many ears of husked sweet corn as desired

Wrap individual ears in plastic wrap. Microwave on HIGH 6-7 minutes per pound (one medium ear weighs 7-8 oz.), rotating the ears halfway through cooking time. Serve with plain or flavored butters (chives and chili powder are this cook's choice).

YOGURT/BERRY PARFAITS

      1 pint frozen vanilla yogurt
      1 cup fresh blueberries
      1 cup fresh red raspberries

Scoop yogurt into footed glasses; surround with the combination of berries. **Yield:** 2-3 servings.

When you have a little more time to barbecue, here's a recipe to try:

PLUM-SAUCED BARBECUED RIBS

Lee Gallahue, Piper City, Illinois

      8 to 10 pounds pork spareribs
SAUCE:
      1/2 cup chopped onion
      2 tablespoons butter
      1 can (17-ounce) purple plums
      1 can (6-ounce) lemonade
        concentrate, thawed
      1/4 cup chili sauce
      1/4 cup reduced-sodium
        soy sauce
      2 teaspoons prepared mustard
      1 teaspoon ground ginger
      1 teaspoon Worcestershire
        sauce

Cut ribs into 3- to 4-rib portions. Place in large kettle with lightly salted water and simmer, covered, for 45 minutes. Drain; set aside. Prepare sauce by cooking onion in butter in pan until clear. Drain plums, reserving liquid. *Remove and discard pits.* Puree plums and reserved liquid until smooth. Add puree to onion/butter mixture; stir in remaining sauce ingredients. Simmer, uncovered, 10-15 minutes, stirring occasionally. Grill ribs over *slow* coals about 25 minutes, turning 3-4 times and brushing with sauce. Serve with remaining sauce. **Yield:** 8-10 servings.

HARVEST SPECIALTIES: Clockwise from lower left—**Spaghetti Sauce**, Nan Banks, Cumberland, Wisconsin (Pg. 62); **Dixie Hen House Eggplant**, Lt./Col. Henry Delaney, Beaumont, Texas (Pg. 62); **Beer Beef Stew**, Marge Reiman, Carroll, Iowa (Pg. 62); **Potato Chowder**, Jane Barta, St. Thomas, North Dakota (Pg. 62); **Potato Kugel**, Marsha Jordan, Harshaw, Wisconsin (Pg. 63); **Sweet Onion Casserole**, Marge Smith, Brawley, California (Pg. 62); **Zucchini Soup**, Charlotte Janeczko, Davenport, Iowa (Pg. 63); **Pennsylvania Corn Soup**, Mildred Sherrer, Bay City, Texas (Pg. 62).

Homegrown goodness is our goal as we fill the harvest table with the flavors of late summer. You can turn your backyard bounty into delicious dishes with these garden-fresh recipes, reflecting the regional tastes of rural America.

Savor a variety of vegetables in a trio of homemade soups, starring tasty blends of corn and peppers, potatoes and carrots or zucchini, onions and herbs. Change the pace with surprising side dishes such as sweet onions with rice, eggplant spiced with sausage or a cheese-topped potato kugel.

Spice up spaghetti with a homemade tomato sauce, or serve up a rich beef vegetable stew...whatever the occasion, these harvesttime helpings are sure to satisfy!

Pick a peach, pear or apple from your orchard or a roadside stand and enjoy the juicy flavors of summer ripening into fall.

And when the fruit ripens fast, tested favorites. You'll find it hard to pick a favorite from fruit-filled Pear Cake, an easy Frozen Peach Cream Pie, an old-fashioned Autumn Apple Tart or a Hidden Gold

FRUIT-FILLED FAVORITES: Clockwise from lower left—**Hidden Gold Cake**, Lucille Drake, Tecumseh, Michigan (Pg. 63); **Autumn Apple Tart**, Grace Howaniec, Waukesha, Wisconsin (Pg. 64); **Pear Cake**, Hazyl Lindley, Abilene, Texas (Pg. 63); **Frozen Peach Cream Pie**, Joann Snyder, Fresno,

FRESH VEGETABLE PIZZA

Jan Hill, Sacramento, California

(PICTURED ON PAGE 52)

TOMATO SAUCE:
- 6 cups fresh tomatoes, Romas preferred
- 2 cloves garlic, minced
- 1/4 teaspoon crushed red pepper flakes
- 1 cup minced onion
- 1/2 teaspoon salt
- 1/2 teaspoon leaf basil, crumbled
- 1 teaspoon leaf oregano, crumbled
- 1 pound frozen bread dough, thawed
- 6 tablespoons grated Parmesan cheese, *divided*
- 1 cup diced green peppers
- 1/2 cup zucchini, julienned (cut in match-stick size)
- 1-1/2 cups grated mozzarella cheese

Olive oil
Assorted toppings—pitted sliced black olives, sliced fresh mushrooms

To make sauce, peel, seed and chop tomatoes; cook in large pan over medium heat until reduced to 3-1/2 cups, about 30 minutes. Stir in remaining sauce ingredients. Simmer for 20 minutes; cool slightly. Set aside. Pat dough into lightly oiled 14-in. pizza pan, pressing up edges to form rim. Cover; let rise 30 minutes. Sprinkle 2 tablespoons Parmesan cheese over crust; spread with tomato sauce. Sprinkle with peppers, zucchini, mozzarella and remaining Parmesan. Top with favorite toppings. Drizzle lightly with olive oil. Bake at 475° for 20 minutes or until crust is golden brown and cheese is melted. **Yield:** 6 servings. **Diabetic Exchanges:** one serving equals 1 protein, 3 bread, 1 vegetable, 1/2 fat; also, 351 calories, 865 mg sodium, 20 mg cholesterol, 50 gm carbohydrate, 18 gm protein, 8 gm fat.

GREEN TOMATO MINCEMEAT

Yvette Knight, New Gloucester, Maine

(PICTURED ON PAGE 52)

- 6 pounds green tomatoes
- 2 pounds tart apples
- 4 cups dark raisins
- 2 cups honey OR 4 cups brown sugar
- 2 cups apple juice OR cider
- 1 lemon, grated rind and juice
- 2 teaspoons grated orange rind
- 1/2 cup cider vinegar
- 1 teaspoon ground nutmeg
- 1 teaspoon ground allspice
- 5 teaspoons cinnamon

Core and quarter tomatoes and apples (*do not peel*). Put through food chopper or use a food processor (chop coarsely). Combine all ingredients in a large non-aluminum kettle. Simmer for 2 hours, stirring frequently until thick. This freezes well or may be processed in jars. To process, pack hot mincemeat into clean, hot, sterilized jars, leaving a 1-in. head space. Adjust lids and process in boiling water bath using the chart below. **Yield:** 7-1/2 pints.

BOILING WATER BATH
Pints and Quarts

Altitude	
	0-1,000 ft.—15 min.
	1,001-6,000 ft.—20 min.
	6,001 ft. and above—25 min.

TOMATOES PROVENCALE

Leatrice Simpkins, Cambridge City, Indiana

(PICTURED ON PAGE 52)

- 4 slices bacon, diced
- 1 clove garlic, minced
- 1 medium onion, thinly sliced
- 1/4 pound fresh mushrooms, sliced
- 1 tablespoon all-purpose flour
- 1/2 teaspoon seasoned salt
- 5 medium tomatoes
- 6 tablespoons grated Parmesan cheese, *divided*
- 1 tablespoon butter

Fry bacon until crisp. Drain on paper towel; *reserve drippings in skillet.* Set aside. Saute garlic, onion and mushrooms in skillet until tender. Stir in reserved bacon, flour and seasoned salt. Set aside. Cut tomatoes into 1/2-in. slices. Place half of the slices in a lightly greased 8-in. square baking dish. Spoon half of bacon/onion mixture over tomatoes. Sprinkle with 3 tablespoons Parmesan cheese. Repeat layers. Dot with butter. Bake at 350° for 25 minutes. **Yield:** 6 servings. **Diabetic Exchanges:** One serving equals 1/2 protein, 1/2 bread, 1 vegetable, 1/2 fat; also, 124 calories, 308 mg sodium, 13 mg cholesterol, 11 gm carbohydrate, 6 gm protein, 6 gm fat.

KANSAS TACO SAUCE

Nila Miller, Frankfort, Kansas

(PICTURED ON PAGE 52)

- 20 large tomatoes, skinned, quartered and mashed
- 4 large onions, chopped
- 4 carrots, cut coarsely
- 3 green peppers
- 5 hot peppers
- 1/2 cup parsley
- 3 tablespoons sugar
- 2 tablespoons salt
- 1 teaspoon pepper
- 3 tablespoons basil
- 1 teaspoon cumin

Bottled lemon juice*

Bring all ingredients *except lemon juice* to a boil in large saucepan; simmer until mixture is desired consistency. (If mixture is too coarse, blend slightly in blender or food processor.) Pour into clean, sterilized jars, adding lemon juice (1 tablespoon/pint; 2 tablespoons/quart) to each jar. *Lemon juice is added to increase acidity. Stir in gently. Seal jars. Taco sauce may be processed by either boiling water bath or pressure canner using the table below. **Yield:** 5 pints.

BOILING WATER BATH

Pints:	Quarts:
Altitude	
0-1,000 ft.—35 min.	Add 5 min. more
1,001-3,000—40 min.	for each
3,001-6,000—45 min.	altitude change.
6,001-8,000—50 min.	

PRESSURE CANNER (Dial Gauge)

Pints: 20 min.	Quarts: 10 min.
Altitude	
0-2,000 ft.—6 lbs.	16 lbs. pressure
2,001-4,000—7 lbs.	(not recommended
4,001-6,000—8 lbs.	at altitudes
6,001-8,000—9 lbs.	above 2,000 ft.)

TOMATO TIPS: To can 1 pint of tomatoes, plan to use 1-1/4 to 1-3/4 lbs. of fresh tomatoes. For 1 pint of juice, allow 1-1/2 to 2 lbs. of tomatoes. • For best flavor, store tomatoes at room temperature. • Tomatoes can be ripened and kept for weeks by wrapping individually in newspaper. • Place unripened tomatoes with other fruit, especially pears, to speed up ripening.

CORN AND TOMATO CASSEROLE
Edna Hoffman, Hebron, Indiana

(PICTURED ON PAGE 53)

3 strips *lean* bacon
1/3 cup minced onion
3 tablespoons green pepper, diced
3 large ears sweet corn (about 3 cups) OR 1 package (16 ounces) frozen sweet corn
2 tablespoons brown sugar (optional)
1 teaspoon salt
1/8 teaspoon pepper
1 teaspoon sweet basil
2-1/2 cups home-canned tomatoes, drained and chopped

TOPPING:
2/3 cup herb-flavored stuffing mix
2/3 cup grated cheddar cheese

In a large skillet, fry bacon until crisp. Drain on paper towel, *reserving the drippings in skillet.* Crumble bacon into bottom of a greased 1-1/2 qt. casserole. Add onions and green pepper to bacon drippings; cook over medium heat until tender. Cut corn off cob; add to onion mixture along with brown sugar, salt, pepper, basil and tomatoes. Cook 10-15 minutes. Pour over bacon in casserole. Top with stuffing mix and cheese. Bake at 350° for 30 minutes. **Yield: 6 servings. Diabetic Exchanges:** 1 bread, 2 vegetable, 1-1/2 fat; also, 185 calories, 459 mg sodium, 20 mg cholesterol, 23 gm carbohydrate, 7 gm protein, 9 gm fat.

SWEET TOMATO PIE
Rita Futral, Ocean Springs, Mississippi

(PICTURED ON PAGE 53)

SPAGHETTI CRUST:
1 package (7 ounces) spaghetti, cooked and drained
2 tablespoons butter, melted
1/2 cup fresh Parmesan cheese, grated
1 egg, beaten

FILLING:
1 pound sweet Italian sausage
1 clove garlic, minced
1 small zucchini, peeled and chopped
1/2 cup (8 medium) green onions, chopped *with tops*
1/2 cup (4 large) fresh mushrooms, chopped
2 tablespoons chopped fresh parsley, *no stems*
5 medium fresh tomatoes, peeled and finely chopped
1/2 teaspoon salt
1/4 teaspoon ground pepper
1/2 to 1 teaspoon Italian seasoning
1 cup mozzarella cheese, grated or cubed

Mix well spaghetti, butter, Parmesan cheese and egg. Spread evenly in well-greased 9-in. to 10-in. pie pan. Remove sausage from casings; crumble into a large skillet. Add the garlic, zucchini, onions, mushrooms and parsley; cook until sausage is no longer pink. Add tomatoes, salt, pepper and Italian seasoning. Mix well. Simmer for 5 minutes, stirring occasionally. Add mozzarella cheese; mix well. Spread meat mixture evenly over spaghetti. Bake at 350° for 25 minutes. Cut in wedges. **Yield:** 6 servings.

HOT CHICKEN, WILD RICE AND TOMATO SALAD
Jeanette Strobel, Brainerd, Minnesota

(PICTURED ON PAGE 53)

4 tablespoons butter
1/2 cup chopped onion
1/2 cup diced celery
2 cups cooked, cubed chicken
2 cups cooked (2/3 cup raw) wild ride OR white rice
1 cup cooked fresh OR frozen peas
2 tablespoons snipped parsley
1 teaspoon *instant* chicken bouillon
1/2 cup boiling water
Salt to taste
Pepper to taste
1/4 to 1/2 teaspoon leaf basil, crumbled
1 cup *toasted* pecans
4 medium ripe tomatoes, cubed

Melt butter in 10-in. skillet or wok. Add onion and celery; saute until tender. Add chicken, wild rice/rice, peas and parsley to skillet. Cook, tossing lightly, until all ingredients are hot. Dissolve bouillon in water; add salt, pepper and basil. Sprinkle over ingredients in skillet. Remove from heat. Add pecans and tomatoes, tossing to blend ingredients. Serve immediately while warm. **Yield:** 6 servings. **Diabetic Exchanges:** One serving equals 2 protein, 1 bread, 3 vegetable, 3 fat; also, 398 caloies, 547 mg sodium, 60 mg cholesterol, 30 gm carbohydrate, 21 gm protein, 23 gm fat.

GREEN TOMATO CHOCOLATE CAKE
Dorothy Kubota, Sacramento, California

(PICTURED ON PAGE 53)

2/3 cup butter
1-3/4 cups sugar
3 eggs, room temperature
2 teaspoons vanilla
2 teaspoons grated orange rind
1/2 cup unsweetened cocoa
2-1/2 cups flour
2 teaspoons baking powder
2 teaspoons baking soda
1 teaspoon salt
1 teaspoon cinnamon
1 cup cultured buttermilk
1 cup (about 3 medium tomatoes) pureed *seeded* green tomatoes
1 cup broken pecans

GLAZE:
2 cups confectioners' sugar
3 tablespoons orange juice
Grated rind from 1 orange

In medium bowl, cream together butter and sugar until light and fluffy. Add eggs, one at a time, beating well after each addition. Stir in vanilla and orange peel; set aside. Combine cocoa, flour, baking powder, soda, salt and cinnamon. Alternately stir flour mixture, buttermilk and tomatoes into egg mixture. Fold in pecans. Turn into a greased and lightly floured bundt *or* tube pan. Bake at 350° for 1 hour or until cake tests done when wooden pick is inserted in center. Invert onto rack to cool completely. Meanwhile, make glaze by combining confectioners' sugar, juice and rind in small bowl. Mix well. Drizzle over cooled cake. **Yield:** 12 servings.

MARINATED HERBED TOMATO SALAD
Frieda Meding, Trochu, Alberta

(PICTURED ON PAGE 54)

6 ripe tomatoes, cut in wedges
3 sweet peppers (combination green, red and yellow), sliced or chunked
1 sweet Spanish onion (white or red), sliced
1 cup pitted black olives

DRESSING:
2/3 cup vegetable oil
1/4 cup vinegar
1/4 cup fresh parsley, snipped
1/4 cup green onions with tops, snipped

1 teaspoon salt
1/4 teaspoon pepper
1 teaspoon sugar
1/2 teaspoon dried basil
(use fresh if available)
1/2 teaspoon dried marjoram
(use fresh if available)

Slice vegetables into glass serving bowl; add olives. Set aside. Combine dressing ingredients in screw-top jar; shake well. Pour over vegetables. Cover and refrigerate for 3-4 hours. **Yield:** 6 servings.

✓ FRESH TOMATO SOUP
Rosemarie Johnson, Norridge, Illinois

(PICTURED ON PAGE 54)
1 cup (2 stalks) chopped celery
1 small onion, chopped
1 carrot, grated
1/2 green pepper, chopped
1/4 cup butter
4-1/2 cups chicken broth, *divided*
1 quart fresh tomatoes, peeled and chopped
1/2 teaspoon curry powder
1/2 teaspoon salt
1/4 teaspoon pepper
4 teaspoons sugar
1/4 cup flour

Saute celery, onion, carrot and green pepper in butter in large heavy pan. Add 4 cups broth, tomatoes, curry powder, salt, pepper and sugar; heat to boiling. Reduce heat; simmer for 20 minutes. Blend flour with remaining 1/2 cup broth. Stir gradually into soup. Cook until slightly thickened, stirring frequently. Serve hot. **Yield:** 2 quarts. **Diabetic Exchanges:** One cup serving equals 1/2 bread, 1/2 fat; also, 57 calories, 368 mg sodium, 9 mg cholesterol, 7 gm carbohydrate, 1 gm protein, 3 gm fat.

APPETIZER TOMATO CHEESE BREAD
Penney Kester, Springville, New York

(PICTURED ON PAGE 54)
SOUR CREAM TOPPING:
1 medium onion, minced
2 tablespoons butter
1/2 cup dairy sour cream
1/4 cup mayonnaise
4 ounces grated cheddar cheese (about 1 cup)
3/4 teaspoon salt
1/4 teaspoon pepper
1/4 teaspoon leaf oregano

Pinch leaf sage
2/3 cup milk
2 cups biscuit mix
3 medium tomatoes, peeled, seeded and sliced 1/4 inch thick
Paprika

Prepare sour cream topping by sauteing onion in butter until tender. Blend with remaining topping ingredients; set aside. Stir milk into biscuit mix to make a soft dough. Turn dough onto a well-floured board; knead lightly for 10 to 12 strokes. Pat dough over bottom of buttered 13-in. x 9-in. x 2-in. baking pan, pushing dough up sides of dish to form a shallow rim. Arrange tomato slices over dough. Spoon on topping; sprinkle with paprika. Bake at 400° for 25 minutes. Let stand 10 minutes before cutting. **Yield:** 12 servings.

STUFFED CHERRY TOMATOES
Donna Smith, Grey Cliff, Montana

(PICTURED ON PAGE 54)
1 pint small cherry tomatoes
FILLING:
1 package (3 ounces) cream cheese, softened
1/4 cup ranch-style dressing
2 tablespoons thinly sliced green onions
2 tablespoons finely chopped water chestnuts
2 tablespoons finely chopped walnuts

Slice off tops of tomatoes. Scoop out pulp with small melon ball cutter, *reserving pulp* to use as necessary to thin filling. Drain tomatoes, upside-down, on paper towel. Combine filling ingredients in small bowl. Stuff tomatoes with filling. Keep refrigerated until serving time. **Yield:** About 24 appetizer tomatoes.

MICROWAVE CHEESY CRUMB TOMATOES
Violet Knoll, Lodi, California

4 tomatoes
1/3 cup dry bread crumbs
2 tablespoons butter
2 tablespoons grated Parmesan cheese
1/2 teaspoon salt
Dash pepper

Cut the tomatoes in half crosswise;

arrange cut side up on microwaveable plate. Set aside. In small bowl, combine bread crumbs and butter; microwave on HIGH, uncovered, for 3-4 minutes or until golden brown/stirring frequently. Stir in cheese and seasonings. Sprinkle crumb mixture over each tomato half. Microwave on HIGH, uncovered, for 3-4 minutes or until hot. **Yield:** 4 servings.

TOMATO CHEESE PIE
Mavis Diment, Marcus, Iowa

4 cups *seasoned* croutons
2 medium tomatoes, sliced
1/4 cup diced green pepper
2 eggs
1-1/2 cups milk
1 teaspoon salt
1/2 teaspoon white pepper
1/2 teaspoon paprika
1/2 teaspoon basil
1/2 teaspoon dry mustard
2 cups shredded Swiss cheese

Pour croutons into a 9-in. pie pan. Slice tomatoes lengthwise and layer on top of the croutons. Mix green pepper, eggs, milk, salt, pepper, paprika, basil and mustard together and pour over tomatoes. Sprinkle on cheese. Bake at 350° for 40 minutes or until brown and puffy. **Yield:** 6 servings.

ICY-HOT TOMATO SALAD
Darlene Smith, Rockford, Illinois

6 large ripe tomatoes
1 large green pepper
1 onion
DRESSING:
3/4 cup cider vinegar
1/4 cup cold water
2 tablespoons sugar
2 teaspoons celery salt
1/8 teaspoon cayenne
1/4 teaspoon black pepper
2 teaspoons dill weed
1 cucumber, sliced (optional)

Peel and quarter tomatoes. Slice green pepper into strips. Cut onion into rings. Place all in a 2-qt. refrigerator container. Combine dressing ingredients in small saucepan; bring to boil while stirring. Boil for 1 minute. Pour over vegetables. Sprinkle dill weed on top. Cover and refrigerate. Before serving, place cucumber slices on top of salad if desired. (Salad will keep several days in refrigerator.) **Yield:** 10-12 servings.

DIXIE HEN HOUSE EGGPLANT

Lt./Col. Henry Delaney, Beaumont, Texas

(PICTURED ON PAGE 56)

3 large eggplants
1/2 pound *spicy* bulk sausage
3 green onions, chopped
1 cup onions, chopped
1 cup celery, chopped
1 package (6-1/4 ounces) corn-bread stuffing mix
1/2 teaspoon black pepper flakes
1/2 teaspoon salt
2 cups grated cheddar cheese

Peel and dice eggplant; cook in salted water until tender. Drain well and set aside. Saute sausage in skillet until well done; remove to paper towels; set aside. Saute green onions, onions and celery in skillet until transparent; set aside. Prepare stuffing mix according to package instructions. Combine eggplant, sausage, onion/celery mixture, salt, pepper and stuffing mix. Transfer to shallow baking dish. Top with cheese; broil until cheese is melted. Serve hot. **Yield:** 12 servings.

SPAGHETTI SAUCE

Nan Banks, Cumberland, Wisconsin

(PICTURED ON PAGE 56)

75 plum tomatoes *or* 50 medium-sized regular tomatoes
1/4 cup brown sugar
2 tablespoons salt
1/2 teaspoon pepper
3 large onions, chopped
6 cloves garlic
3/4 cup fresh parsley *or* 1/4 cup dried parsley flakes
1 tablespoon dried basil leaves *or* 3 tablespoons fresh
1 tablespoon dried oregano leaves *or* 3 tablespoons fresh
1 tablespoon dried thyme *or* 3 tablespoons fresh
3 bay leaves

Wash, core and halve tomatoes. (If using regular tomatoes, drain in colander after quartering and squeeze gently to remove seeds and excess juice before cooking.) In 12-quart kettle combine tomatoes, brown sugar, salt, pepper. Bring to boil, stirring occasionally. Reduce heat and boil gently, uncovered, for 1 hour. Add remaining ingredients; boil gently, stirring occasionally for 1 hour or until the sauce reaches the

desired consistency. Puree through food mill. Pour hot sauce into sterilized hot pint jars, leaving 1-inch head space. Adjust lids. Process in pressure canner at 10 pounds for 35 minutes. (One tablespoon cornstarch, diluted in water, added to 1 quart of sauce before reheating will thicken sauce perfectly.)

BEER BEEF STEW

Marge Reiman, Carroll, Iowa

(PICTURED ON PAGE 57)

1 pound boneless chuck roast, cut in 1-inch cubes
1 can (10-3/4 ounces) sodium-reduced cream of mushroom soup
1 package dry onion soup mix
1 soup can beer
1 cup canned tomatoes, drained or 3 fresh tomatoes, peeled and quartered
6 small whole onions *or* 1 small can pearl onions, drained
4 to 6 medium potatoes, peeled & quartered
2 to 3 ribs celery, sliced in 2-inch chunks
2 to 3 carrots, sliced in 2-inch chunks
1 teaspoon Worcestershire sauce

Combine meat, soup, onion soup mix and beer in oven-proof casserole or Dutch oven with tight-fitting lid. Cover; bake at 300° for 3 hours. Add tomatoes, onions, potatoes, celery, carrots and Worcestershire sauce; return to oven for 1 hour or longer. **Yield:** 6-8 servings.

PENNSYLVANIA CORN SOUP

Mildred Sherrer, Bay City, Texas

(PICTURED ON PAGE 57)

1 cup sweet red pepper, finely chopped
1 cup finely chopped onion
4 teaspoons corn oil
2 teaspoons butter
4 teaspoons whole wheat flour
2 cups milk
3 cups fresh *or* 1 package (16 ounces) frozen corn, *divided*
1 cup light cream *or* half-and-half
4 teaspoons tamari*
Dash nutmeg
Parsley for garnish

*Tamari is available at health food stores or Oriental markets. In large saucepan, cook the pepper and onion in oil and butter until tender. Stir in the flour and continue stirring over low heat for 2-3 minutes. Add milk slowly, stirring after each addition to prevent lumping. Set aside. Place *1 cup* corn, cream and tamari in blender. Process on medium speed until fairly smooth. Add corn/cream mixture and remaining corn to the milk mixture. Heat thoroughly and serve topped with a dash of nutmeg. Garnish with parsley. **Yield:** 4 servings.

POTATO CHOWDER

Jane Barta, St. Thomas, North Dakota

(PICTURED ON PAGE 57)

4 cups peeled, diced potatoes
1/2 cup finely chopped onion
1 cup grated carrot
1 teaspoon salt
1/4 teaspoon pepper
1 tablespoon dried parsley flakes
4 chicken bouillon cubes
6 cups scalded milk
4 tablespoons butter
1/2 cup flour

In large Dutch oven or kettle, combine potatoes, onion, carrot, salt, pepper, parsley flakes and bouillon cubes. Add enough water to just cover vegetables; cook until vegetables are tender, about 15-20 minutes. *Do not drain.* Scald milk by heating to 180° or until tiny bubbles form around edges of pan. Remove 1-1/2 cups milk and add butter and flour to hot milk, stirring with wire whisk. Add remaining hot milk to undrained vegetables, then stir in thickened milk mixture. Stir until blended. Simmer for 15 minutes on low heat. **Yield:** 8-10 servings.

SWEET ONION CASSEROLE

Marge Smith, Brawley, California

(PICTURED ON PAGE 57)

1/2 cup long grain rice, *uncooked*
7 to 8 cups Imperial sweet onions, chopped coarsely
1/4 cup melted butter
1 cup grated Swiss cheese
2/3 cup half-and-half
1 teaspoon salt

Cook rice in 5 cups boiling water for

5 minutes. Drain; set aside. Cook onions in butter in large skillet until limp but not browned. Combine all ingredients, mix well and pour into greased 2-qt. casserole. Bake at 350° for 1 hour. **Yield: 8-10 servings.**

ZUCCHINI SOUP

Charlotte Janeczko, Davenport, Iowa

(PICTURED ON PAGE 57)

  3 slices lean bacon, cut in small
     pieces
  1 medium onion, chopped
  1 clove garlic, minced
  8 medium zucchini, cut in
     1/2-inch slices (about 8
     cups)
  1 can (10-1/2 ounces) beef
     consomme
2-1/2 cups water
  1 teaspoon salt
  4 tablespoons fresh parsley
  1 teaspoon dried basil leaves
     (can use fresh)
1/8 teaspoon pepper
Freshly grated Parmesan cheese
Bacon bits for garnish, if desired

Brown bacon pieces in large skillet; pour off all but 1 tablespoon bacon fat. Stir onion and garlic in fat until onion is tender. Add remaining ingredients *except cheese* .Bring to a boil, then simmer, uncovered, until zucchini is tender, about 20 minutes. Pour soup into blender, about 2 cups at a time. Cover; blend on low speed until liquified, then blend on high until smooth. Serve hot or cold with Parmesan cheese and additional bacon bits. **Yield: 8 one-cup servings.**

POTATO KUGEL

Marsha Jordan, Harshaw, Wisconsin

(PICTURED ON PAGE 57)

  6 medium-sized russet
     potatoes, peeled
  2 to 3 carrots, peeled
  1 onion
  1 clove garlic, minced
  2 beaten eggs
  3 tablespoons vegetable oil
  2 teaspoons salt
1/4 cup *whole grain* bread
     crumbs

3/4 cup powdered non-fat milk
TOPPING:
  1 cup cheddar cheese, grated
  1 cup plain yogurt *or* sour
     cream
Fresh chives for garnish, if desired

Grate vegetables; drain off liquid. Stir in remaining ingredients except topping, adding milk powder gradually to avoid any lumps. Spread into greased 7-inch x 11-inch baking pan. (Can also use 9-inch square pan with additional baking time.) Bake at 350° for 40-60 minutes. When kugel is nearly done it will test dry like a cake and the edges will be brown. Add grated cheese and return to oven for 5 more minutes until cheese melts. Remove from oven; cut into 2-inch squares. Top each square with about 2 tablespoons yogurt/sour cream. Garnish with fresh chives, if desired. **Yield: 6-8 servings.**

FROZEN PEACH CREAM PIE

Joann Snyder, Fresno, California

(PICTURED ON PAGE 58)

  1 can (14 ounces) sweetened
     condensed milk
Juice of 2 large lemons, about
     1/2 cup
  1 cup heavy cream, whipped
  2 cups fresh ripe peaches,
     sliced and cut into small
     pieces
  1 9-inch graham cracker crust*

Mix milk with lemon juice (mixture will thicken). Fold thickened mixture into whipped cream and peaches. Pour into chilled crust. Freeze until firm. Serve frozen. (Can also use raspberries, boysenberries, strawberries or fresh apricots in place of peaches.) *May make in springform pan, as shown.

PEAR CAKE

Hazyl Lindley, Abilene, Texas

(PICTURED ON PAGE 58)

  2 cups sugar
1-1/2 cups vegetable oil
  3 eggs
  3 cups flour
  1 teaspoon cinnamon
  1 teaspoon salt
  1 teaspoon baking soda
  2 teaspoons vanilla

  2 cups flaked coconut, about 1
     (7 ounce) package
  1 cup chopped dates
  3 cups raw *or* canned pears,
     drained and chopped
  1 cup pecans, chopped, about 1
     (4 ounce) package

Cream together sugar and oil. Add eggs, one at a time, mixing well after each addition. Set aside. Sift flour with cinnamon, salt and soda 3 times, then add to creamed mixture. Add vanilla; mix. Add coconut, dates, pears and pecans, stirring by hand (batter will be thick). Pour into greased and floured bundt pan. Bake at 325° for 1-1/2 to 2 hours or until cake tests done with a wooden pick inserted in center. Cool on rack until cake shrinks from sides of pan; remove from pan to complete cooling. **Yield: 16 servings.**

HIDDEN GOLD CAKE

Lucille Drake, Tecumseh, Michigan

(PICTURED ON PAGE 58)

  2 cups sugar
  2 cups flour
  2 teaspoons baking soda
  1 teaspoon salt
  1 cup vegetable oil
  4 eggs, room temperature
  3 cups finely grated raw
     carrots, packed (about 1
     pound)
Lemon frosting or filling*

Mix sugar, flour, baking soda and salt. Add oil; mix well. Add eggs, one at a time, beating well after each addition. Stir in carrots. Pour batter into greased and paper-lined 13- x 9- x 1-inch jelly roll pan or three greased and floured 8-inch layer cake pans. Bake at 350° for 20 minutes for jelly roll or 35 minutes or until cake tests done for layers. (Do not open oven door for first 20 to 30 minutes of baking time.) Loosen edges of cake in jelly roll pan as soon as it is removed from oven. Reverse pan onto a clean towel that has been dusted with confectioners' sugar. Roll up in towel and place on rack to cool. When thoroughly cool, unroll cake to fill and top with favorite lemon frosting or filling. Let layer cake cool in pans for 10 minutes; remove to cake rack. *We used a cooled lemon meringue pie filling combined with chilled whipped cream as a filling.

AUTUMN APPLE TART

Grace Howaniec, Food Editor

(PICTURED ON PAGE 58)

CRUST:
1-1/4 cups all-purpose flour
1 teaspoon baking powder
1/2 teaspoon salt
1 tablespoon sugar
1/2 cup butter *or* margarine
1 egg, beaten
2 tablespoons milk
6 medium baking apples, peeled, cored and sliced 1/4 inch thick (use Granny Smith or Jonathan, if possible)

TOPPING:
1/3 to 1/2 cup sugar
2 tablespoons butter *or* margarine
1/2 teaspoon ground cinnamon
1/2 teaspoon ground nutmeg
1-1/2 tablespoons all-purpose flour

Make crust by combining flour, baking powder, salt and sugar in medium-sized bowl. Cut in butter/margarine with pastry blender until mixture resembles fine crumbs. Combine egg and milk; add to flour/butter mixture. Stir to blend. With lightly floured hands, press dough into a 12-in. diameter tart pan (with removable bottom). Press dough up sides to form a 1-in. rim. (May use a 13-inch x 9-inch x 2-inch baking pan instead of tart pan.) Fill tart shell with overlapping apple slices, beginning at outer edge. See diagram. Combine topping ingredients; sprinkle evenly over apples. Bake at 350° for 50-60 minutes until apples are fork-tender. Cut in wedges; serve warm or cool. **Yield:** 12 servings.

PUMPKIN TORTE

Mrs. Larry Steinke, Burlington, Wisconsin

24 graham crackers, crushed
1/3 cup sugar
1/2 cup butter
2 eggs, beaten
3/4 cup sugar
1 package (8-ounce) cream cheese
2 cups cooked pumpkin
3 egg yolks
1/2 cup sugar
1/2 cup milk
1/2 teaspoon salt
1 tablespoon cinnamon
1 envelope plain gelatin

1/4 cup cold water
3 egg whites
1/4 cup sugar
1/2 pint whipping cream

Mix graham cracker crumbs, 1/3 cup sugar and butter and press into 9- x 13-in. pan. Mix eggs, 3/4 cup sugar and cream cheese; pour over crust. Bake 20 minutes at 350°. Cook pumpkin, egg yolks, 1/2 cup sugar, milk, salt and cinnamon until mixture thickens. Remove from heat; add gelatin which has been dissolved in cold water. Cool. Beat egg whites, 1/4 cup sugar and fold in pumpkin mixture. Pour over cooled baked crust. Top with whipped cream. **Yield:** 16 servings.

GOURMET POTATOES

Eula Riggins, Odon, Indiana

6 medium-sized potatoes
1/4 cup butter
2 cups shredded cheddar cheese
1/2 cup cultured sour cream
1 tablespoon minced onion
1 teaspoon salt
1/4 teaspoon ground pepper
2 tablespoons butter
Paprika

Cook unpeeled potatoes until tender. Cool, peel and shred coarsely. Heat butter in saucepan; remove from heat. Add cheese, stirring until partially melted. Blend in sour cream, onion, salt and pepper; fold in potatoes. Place in greased 2-qt. casserole dish; dot with 2 tablespoons butter. Sprinkle with paprika. Bake, uncovered, at 350° for 30 minutes or until nicely browned. NOTE: Casserole may be assembled day before; if you do, cover and refrigerate, and lengthen cooking time. **Yield:** 8-10 servings.

BANANA SPLIT DESSERT

Mrs. Elmer Thorsheim, Radcliffe, Iowa

5 cups graham cracker crumbs
2/3 cup butter, melted
2 to 3 bananas
1/2 gallon Neapolitan ice cream
1 cup chopped walnuts
1 cup chocolate chips

1/2 cup butter
2 cups confectioners' sugar
1-1/2 cups evaporated milk
1 teaspoon vanilla
1 pint whipping cream

Prepare crust from crumbs and 2/3 cup butter; reserve 1 cup crumbs. Press remaining crumb mixture into bottom of 11- x 15-in. baking pan. Slice bananas crosswise and layer over crust. Cut ice cream in 1/2-in.-thick slices; place over bananas. Sprinkle ice cream with 1 cup chopped walnuts. Freeze until firm. Melt 1 cup chocolate chips and 1/2 cup butter; add 2 cups confectioners' sugar and evaporated milk. Cook mixture until thick and smooth, stirring constantly. Remove from heat; add vanilla. Cool chocolate mixture; pour over ice cream. Freeze until firm. Whip cream until stiff; spread over chocolate layer; top with reserved crumbs. Store in freezer; remove about 10 minutes before serving. (Will keep for several weeks.) **Yield:** 25 servings.

SANTA FE ENCHILADAS

Barbara Beichley, Gladbrook, Iowa

1-1/2 pounds ground beef OR pork
1 can (12 ounces) tomato paste
1 cup water
1/2 cup chopped onion
1 package taco seasoning mix, optional
Salt, if desired
12 flour tortillas
1 jar (8 ounces) Cheese Whiz
1 can (4 ounces) chopped green chili peppers, drained

Crumble meat in large mixing bowl; microwave on HIGH 6-8 minutes or until meat loses pink color. Drain. Add paste, water, onion, taco seasoning (if desired) and salt to meat; microwave on HIGH 3 minutes. Set aside. Wrap tortillas in dampened paper towels and MICROWAVE on HIGH 1-2 minutes until soft. Spoon 2 tablespoons meat mixture on each tortilla; roll up tightly. Place in lightly greased 9- x 13-in. baking dish. Combine Cheese Whiz and green chilies; microwave on HIGH for 1-2 minutes until heated through. Pour over tortillas. Top with remaining meat mixture. Microwave on HIGH 5 minutes; rotate dish. Cover with plastic wrap; microwave on HIGH 5 minutes more. Let stand, covered, 5 minutes. **Yield:** 10-12 servings.

ROUND STEAK SUPREME

Marla Wittkamper, Elwood, Indiana

2-1/2 pounds round steak
1/2 cup flour
2 eggs
1/2 cup milk
1 cup fine crumbs (cracker OR bread)
1/2 cup grated Parmesan cheese
1/2 teaspoon ground pepper
1/4 cup parsley flakes
1 teaspoon garlic salt
1 teaspoon onion salt
2 tablespoons vegetable oil
Fresh ripe tomatoes OR firm whole canned, drained
1/2 cup water

Cut meat into 1-in. squares; coat with flour. Beat eggs and milk in flat dish. Combine crumbs, cheese, pepper, parsley and garlic and onion salt on paper plate. Dip meat into egg mixture, then roll in crumbs. Brown meat in hot oil. Place in 2-qt. baking dish. Arrange tomato slices over meat. Stir water into drippings in skillet; heat to boiling, scraping brown bits from pan. Pour over meat. Cover and bake at 325° 1-1/2 hours. **Yield:** 6 servings.

✓ ONE-STEP CHILI

Lois Schierbeek, Holland, Michigan

1 pound lean ground beef
1 can (15 ounces) pinto OR kidney beans plus liquid
1 can (14-1/2 ounces) whole tomatoes and juice, cut up
1 can (6 ounces) tomato paste
1/2 cup chopped onion
1/4 cup chopped green pepper
1 garlic clove, crushed
2 tablespoons chili powder
1 teaspoon salt
1/2 teaspoon ground cumin
1/4 teaspoon red pepper flakes, optional

Microwave crumbled ground beef in 2-qt. casserole on HIGH for 5 minutes, stirring once to break meat into pieces. Drain. Add remaining ingredients. Cover; microwave on HIGH for

20 minutes, stirring every 5 minutes. **Yield:** 6 servings. **Diabetic Exchanges:** One serving equals 2 protein, 1 bread, 2 vegetables, 1 fat; also, 252 calories, 541 mg sodium, 69 mg cholesterol, 23 mg carbohydrate.

OPEN-FACED TUNA LOAF

Sara Tatham, Plymouth, New Hampshire

1 large loaf Italian bread
Butter, softened
6 to 8 ounces Monterey Jack cheese, sliced thin
2 cans (6-1/2 ounces) tuna, drained
1/3 to 1/2 cup mayonnaise
1/4 cup chopped parsley (reserve 1 tablespoon for garnish)
Dash of pepper
1 tablespoon lemon juice

Slice bread in half lengthwise; butter both halves. Place bread, buttered side up, in 13- x 9-in. glass pan. Cover both halves of bread with cheese slices. Mix remaining ingredients together, adjusting mayonnaise to taste. Spread on top of cheese-covered bread. Microwave on HIGH for 6 to 7 minutes, rotating dish after 3 minutes. Sprinkle with reserved parsley. **Yield:** 8 servings. **Conventional Method:** Broil 3 inches from heat for about 10 minutes or until lightly browned.

✓ CALICO-STUFFED PEPPERS

Joann Krebs, Juniata, Nebraska

3 large green peppers, halved lengthwise, seeded, membrane removed
1 pound *extra* lean ground beef
3/4 cup chopped onion
1 can (8 ounces) whole kernel corn
3 tablespoons catsup
1/4 teaspoon garlic powder
1/2 teaspoon chili powder
1 can (8 ounces) tomato sauce
1 teaspoon chili powder
1/2 cup grated cheddar cheese

Arrange peppers in 4-qt. casserole or on 14-in. round glass tray. Cover with plastic wrap, turning back one corner to vent steam. Microwave on HIGH 4 minutes. Set aside. In 2-qt. casserole, crumble beef and add onion. Microwave on HIGH 5 minutes, stirring once. Drain. Add corn, catsup, garlic and 1/2 teaspoon chili powder to

beef. Mix; spoon into pepper shells. Combine tomato sauce and 1 teaspoon chili powder; spoon over pepper halves. Cover; microwave on HIGH 5 minutes. Sprinkle with cheese; microwave on HIGH, uncovered, 1 minute. Let stand 2 minutes before serving. **Yield:** 6 servings: **Diabetic Exchanges:** One serving equals 2 protein, 1 bread, 1 vegetable; also, 247 calories, 524 mg sodium, 92 mg cholesterol, 18 gm carbohydrate.

CORN CHOWDER

Lois DeVries, Worthing, South Dakota

1 cup chopped onion
1/2 cup chopped celery
2 tablespoons butter, melted
3 cups corn, fresh OR frozen
1-1/2 cups peeled, cubed potatoes
1-1/2 cups water
3 chicken-flavored bouillon cubes
1 teaspoon salt
1/4 teaspoon pepper
1/4 teaspoon dried thyme
2 cups milk, divided
2 tablespoons flour
1 cup half and half OR cream

Combine onion, celery and butter in 3-qt. casserole; microwave on HIGH for 2 minutes. Add corn, potatoes, water, bouillon, salt, pepper and thyme and microwave on HIGH until potatoes are tender, about 10 minutes. Heat 1 cup milk and 2 tablespoons flour to boiling; stir into soup. Add remaining milk and half and half/cream. Microwave until thoroughly heated. **Yield:** 6 servings.

SPEEDY GROUND BEEF: *Cook and drain 1 lb. ground beef simultaneously by microwaving in a microwave-safe colander set inside a deep casserole dish. Microwave 4-6 minutes on HIGH; stirring with fork to break up meat every 2 minutes.*

NATURAL HARVEST CENTERPIECE: *Use a small pumpkin for the base of your autumn table decoration. Carve it out, scallop the opening, set a water-filled container inside and fill it with tiny cattails, dried weeds and the last of your rust and yellow chrysanthemums.*

Country Inns

The Brick House
Bed & Breakfast

**The Brick House
Bed & Breakfast**
Box 301, Goodfield, Illinois 61742
309/965-2545

Directions: from Bloomington, take I-74 West (from Peoria, I-74 East) to Exit #112; Hwy. 117 North, through Goodfield to Timberline Road; east to bed & breakfast and theater.

Owner: Chaunce Conklin

Schedule: Bed & breakfast daily, theater performances Wednesday through Sunday. Closed first 2 weeks in January.

Rates and Accommodations: Four guest rooms with shared baths, $44-$54 double occupancy includes full breakfast. Dinner theater/lodging packages for two people, $68-$78 Wednesday, Thursday and Sunday; $78-$88 Friday and Saturday. Dinner theater only, $17.40-$21.45 per person. Personal checks, no credit cards.

The fare may be down-home, but the surroundings and staff certainly have a flair for the dramatic at The Brick House Bed & Breakfast's Dinner Theatre!

Actors and actresses, dressed in the costumes they'll wear while performing, serve appetizers, soup and beverages. (No liquor is sold here, but patrons may bring in their own cocktails, wine or beer.)

Then guests help themselves to the salad bar, and later to an entree buffet which features such favorites as fried chicken, spaghetti with meat sauce or a tasty round of beef, accompanied by mashed potatoes with gravy, peas and carrots and hot bread. Dessert choices might include cherry cheesecake, turtle brownies and pudding parfait. Other nights, the buffet might include one of chef Bob Mathews' hits, the easy-to-make seafood entree featured below.

Banjo players entertain throughout dinner, then the show begins! The resident theater company's repertoire includes comedy, musical comedy, drama, murder mystery, summer children's theater and an old-fashioned melodrama that has been running every Wednesday evening since the theater opened in 1975.

After the show, guests find that a walk back to the across-the-yard bed and breakfast is a nice convenience— and in the morning they enjoy a hearty country breakfast, such as baked eggs, bacon, blueberry muffins, orange juice and coffee, while chatting about the previous night's show.

Try a few of The Brick House's favorites for yourself:

MAPLE TOAST EGG BAKE

4 day-old bread slices
4 large eggs
3 tablespoons melted butter
3 tablespoons maple syrup

Cut crusts off bread; brush both sides of bread slices with mixture of butter and maple syrup. Place prepared bread in muffin tins or ramekins to form a cup. Place an egg into each bread cup. Bake in a 350° oven until egg is cooked to your liking —12 to 14 minutes for soft yolks. **NOTE:** Eggs will be more cooked on the bottom.

ROQUEFORT DRESSING

3 to 4 ounces crumbled Roquefort cheese (6 tablespoons)
1/8 teaspoon black pepper
1 teaspoon onion salt
1/3 cup garlic wine vinegar
1/4 teaspoon paprika
1/4 teaspoon sugar
4 tablespoons olive oil

Mash cheese with fork. Blend in pepper, onion salt, paprika and sugar. Add vinegar and olive oil; mix thoroughly. Pour over washed, torn salad greens and toss until leaves are coated. **Yield:** 1-1/2 cups dressing.

FRESH FRUIT SAUCE

1 can (20 ounces) pineapple chunks in unsweetened syrup, drained, reserving syrup
1/2 cup sugar
3 tablespoons cornstarch
1/4 cup lemon juice
1/4 cup orange juice
1 teaspoon each lemon and orange rind

Combine pineapple juice, sugar and cornstarch in a medium saucepan; bring to a boil and cook for 1 minute, stirring constantly. Add juices and rind; mix. Chill and pour over any combination of fruit—strawberries, watermelon and muskmelon balls, peaches, pears, pineapple or berries. **Yield:** Approximately 2 cups sauce.

CHEF'S SPAGHETTI FISHERMAN

1 pound thin spaghetti *or* linguine
1/2 pound butter
6 cloves garlic, minced
1 cup fresh mushrooms, sliced
1 cup green onions, chopped (reserve some for garnish)
1 pound medium shrimp, peeled and deveined
1 pound crabmeat
Chopped green onions (garnish)

Cook spaghetti according to package directions; drain and keep warm. In saucepan, melt butter; add garlic and saute. Add mushrooms, green onions, shrimp and crabmeat. Saute just until shrimp turn pink and mixture is hot. Toss with spaghetti. Garnish with green onions. **Yield:** 8 servings.

PINEAPPLE/ COCONUT PIE

1 stick butter, melted
1-1/2 cups sugar
1 cup drained crushed pineapple
1 tablespoon vinegar
1 cup shredded coconut
3 eggs, slightly beaten
1 teaspoon vanilla
1 9-in. *unbaked* pie shell

Mix all ingredients; pour into unbaked pie shell. Bake at 300° for 1 hour.

Best Cook

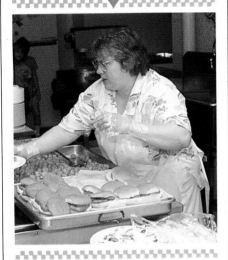

Making meals memorable is something Barbara McDougal does every school day, as she cooks and serves food to nearly 100 students, teachers and visitors at Downs Elementary School in Rachel, West Virginia. Her meals are so good that Janet Cunningham, one of the teachers there, nominated her as "Best Cook in the Country"!

"Downs is a small, rural school with 79 students, almost all of whom eat the hot lunch in our cafeteria every day. Barbara does the preparation and serving, turning out good home-cooked meals complete with rolls, desserts and special treats.

"Barbara takes time to get to know the children, smiling and talking to them as they go through the line. On holidays, she wears costumes—a witch for Halloween or Mrs. Santa Claus at Christmas—and that delights the children."

On "School Cook's Day" the students and staff of Downs honored Barbara by presenting her with a corsage and a book, written by students, titled *Why We Think Our Cook Is Great.* Here are excerpts:

"I like our cook because she is nice and her cooking is terrific. I love her pizza, macaroni and pepperoni rolls. She also gives a lot of whatever she has cooked." —*Shannon Fleeman*

"She's a very nice and sweet cook. She makes things people haven't heard of and tells us to taste it. It turns out good." —*Ashley Hillbury*

BASIC BREAD DOUGH

    5 cups very warm water
    2 eggs, slightly beaten
    1/4 cup instant yeast
    1/8 cup salt
    1 cup sugar
    1 cup oil

    5 pounds flour

Combine water, eggs, yeast, salt, sugar and oil in the order given. Mix. Add 5 lbs. of flour; mix well. If dough is sticky, add a little flour. Knead about 5 minutes. Put into well-oiled bowl and cover with plastic wrap. Let rise in warm place until double. Dough may be shaped into rolls, loaves, pepperoni rolls or pizza crust. **Yield:** 2 loaves, 18 rolls, 24 pepperoni rolls or 2 pizza crusts.

* Pepperoni Roll: Form dough into balls about the size of an egg; flatten with hand and place several slices of pre-sliced pepperoni or two sticks about 2 in. long and 1/4 in. wide in the middle. Roll, closing ends, and place rolled side down in a greased pan. You may also roll whole wieners this way for wiener wraps. Bake at 350° for 20-25 minutes. **Yield:** 18 rolls.

DEER JERKY

    3 pounds venison

    1/2 cup soy sauce
    1/2 cup Worcestershire sauce
    2 teaspoons Accent
    2 teaspoons table salt
    2/3 teaspoon onion powder
    2/3 teaspoon black pepper

Cut venison into 3/4-in. strips. Combine the remaining ingredients; pour over meat and refrigerate, covered, overnight. Drain; hang meat over the racks in your oven and bake at 150° or the lowest setting of your oven for 6 to 8 hours, until meat is dried.

PIZZA SAUCE

    2 tablespoons oil
    1 can (15 ounces) tomato
      puree
    1 can (4-1/2 ounces) tomato
      paste

    1/4 teaspoon parsley flakes
    1/2 teaspoon salt
    1/8 teaspoon pepper
    1/8 teaspoon garlic powder
    1 teaspoon oregano
    1/2 cup water

Combine all ingredients; simmer 10 minutes on low heat. Bake pizza crust with the sauce and pepperoni at 350° for about 10 minutes. Add chopped green pepper, pre-cooked hot Italian sausage, black olives, mushrooms and shredded mozzarella cheese and bake another 10 minutes or until desired brownness. **Yield:** 1 pizza, 12 inches.

STRAWBERRY BANANA NUT BREAD

    1 stick softened margarine
    3 eggs
    1 cup sugar
    1/2 pint fresh strawberries, chopped
    3 medium sliced ripe bananas
    1/2 cup milk
    1/2 cup chopped nuts
    3 cups flour
    4 teaspoons baking powder
    1/2 teaspoon salt

Beat together margarine, eggs and sugar. Stir in strawberries and bananas (strawberries may remain chunky). Add milk, nuts, flour, baking powder and salt. Divide between three 7-3/8-in. x 3-5/8-in x 2-1/4-in. greased loaf pans and bake at 350° for 35-40 minutes. Let cool 1/2 hour before slicing. Spread with butter or eat plain.

PEACH COBBLER

    1/4 pound margarine
    3 cups sliced peaches,
      including syrup
    2 cups flour
    2 teaspoons baking powder
    1 teaspoon salt
    2 cups sugar
    2 cups milk

Melt margarine in bottom of 13-in. x 9-in. x 2-in. pan. Add peaches and syrup to melted butter. Combine remaining ingredients; pour over peaches and margarine. Bake at 350° for 45-50 minutes, or until golden brown. Serve in a bowl with milk and sugar or with ice cream on top. **Yield:** 12 servings.

Fresh from backyard branches or nearby orchard, apples are at the heart of many cherished recipes. And here's a bumper crop of palate-pleasing apple eating!

There's a coffee cake that's so quick to bake you'll find yourself fixing it often each fall...ever-popular apple pie bars...feathery fruit muffins...bewitching bread pudding...cakes of contrasting kinds...a man-pleasing main dish...and an apple pie that's truly a prizewinner.

Bring home a bag or bushel of apples today and put fall at its finest on your table tonight!

AAH...APPLES! Clockwise from far left—**Apple Streusel Coffee Cake**, Laralee Hanes, Troy, Ontario (Pg. 75); **Apple Bread Pudding**, Martha Doyle, Kalispell, Montana (Pg. 75); **Apple Sour Cream Bundt Cake**, Gayle West, Darwin, Minnesota (Pg. 75); **Prize-Winning Apple Pie**, Ruth Unruh, Newton, Kansas (Pg. 76); **Apple Streusel Muffins**, June Isaac, Abbotsford, British Columbia (Pg. 76); **Apple/Sausage/Sweet Potato Casserole**, Irene Gerdes, Red Wing, Minnesota (Pg. 75); **Fresh Apple Cake**, Joan Baskin, Black Creek, British Columbia (Pg. 76); and **Apple Pie Bars**, Cindy Cyr, Fowler, Indiana (Pg. 75).

Appetizing apples—
their crisply sweet crunch and rose-
cheeked cast add color all their
own to autumn!

When apples are at their peak,
take your pick from among these
mouth-watering recipes.

APPLE OF YOUR EYE. Clockwise
from bottom—**Apple Sausage Breakfast Ring**, Cherie Sechrist, Red Lion,
Pennsylvania (Pg. 77); **Apple/Cran-
berry Crisp**, Candie Takacs, West Carrollton, Ohio (Pg. 76); **Fresh Apple
Salad**, Becky Druetzler, Indianapolis,
Indiana (Pg. 76); **Apple, Raisin, Wal-
nut Cake**, Pollie Malone, Ames, Iowa
(Pg. 77).

Recipes from Mary Ellen Agnew, Dundalk, Ontario.

meals in MINUTES

MINUTES matter at mealtime, as any busy cook knows. And when you're looking for fast fare with a seasonal flair, here's a menu to turn to—for delicious results in less than half an hour.

Begin by preparing the lightly seasoned chicken dish (you may want to add some ground white pepper.) Cortland apples are great with the chicken, but McIntosh or Northern Spy work too, depending on availability.

While the chicken simmers, heat water for noodles, clean the green beans and scald and peel the peaches for dessert.

To save time with the dessert, use your own raspberry freezer jam, or frozen or fresh raspberries, dusted with sugar.

CREAMY CHICKEN AND APPLES

- 1 tablespoon vegetable oil
- 4 chicken breast halves, flattened to 1/2-inch thickness
- 1 medium cooking onion, peeled and sliced
- 1/2 cup chicken broth
- 1/4 cup dry white wine OR apple juice OR water
- 1/4 teaspoon leaf thyme
- 1/4 teaspoon salt
- 4 medium red cooking apples, cored and cut in 1/8-inch slices
- 1 tablespoon flour
- 3/4 cup light cream OR evaporated milk

Heat oil in frying pan; saute chicken with onion until golden brown on both sides. Reduce heat; add chicken broth, wine/juice, thyme and salt. Cover; simmer for 10 minutes. Remove chicken from pan; keep warm. Add apples to pan; cover and simmer for 3-5 minutes until apples are fork-tender, stirring occasionally. Dissolve the flour in cream; stir into pan, cook and stir until slightly thickened. Spoon the sauce over chicken. Serve with egg noodles cooked according to package directions. **Yield:** 4 servings.

GARDEN GREEN BEANS

- 1 pound fresh green beans, washed and stemmed
- Water
- Salt
- Butter

Cook beans in medium saucepan in enough boiling salted water until tender/crisp, about 6 minutes. Drain; dot with butter. **Yield:** 4 servings.

QUICK PEACH MELBA

- 4 fresh ripe peaches, peeled and halved
- 1 pint French vanilla ice cream
- 1/2 cup raspberry freezer jam OR sugared frozen or fresh raspberries

Place a peach half in the bottom of a sherbet dish; top with a scoop of ice cram. Drizzle 2 tablespoons (or more if desired) of jam over top of ice cream. Serve with a sugar cookie, if desired. **Yield:** 4 servings.

Here's another chicken dish that's tasty and quick!

✓ CHICKEN PARMESAN

Vonda Miller, Osgood, Indiana

- 1/4 cup butter
- 1/2 cup Parmesan cheese
- 1/2 cup bread crumbs
- 1 tablespoon paprika
- 1/4 to 1/2 teaspoon garlic powder
- 1-1/2 teaspoons Italian seasoning OR 1/2 teaspoon each of rosemary, oregano, basil
- 6 chicken breast *halves*, boned, skinned (1-1/2 pounds)

*Chicken parts may be substituted for chicken breasts—allow 7 minutes per pound of chicken for cooking. Melt butter in 8- x 12-in. glass pan. Dip both sides of chicken in butter. Combine remaining ingredients on paper plate; roll chicken in mixture. Place chicken in dish, with thicker edges toward outside. Cover loosely with waxed paper. Microwave on HIGH for 12 minutes, rotating dish once. **Yield:** 6 servings. **Conventional Method:** Omit waxed paper. Bake at 350° for 35-45 minutes. **Diabetic Exchanges:** One serving equals 3 protein, 1/2 bread, 1 fat; also, 283 calories, 284 mg sodium, 114 mg cholesterol, 7 gm carbohydrate.

71

♥ **P**ack up the pickup (or station wagon) and head for the football field or the neighborhood woods…it's time for a tailgate party!

Fill the picnic basket and coolers with these recipes—they'll make it easy to satisfy hearty appetites whetted by autumn's crisp air and cooler temperatures.

Start with a thermos filled with hot mulled cider. Tuck in a spicy popcorn snack. Add some substantial main dishes, including meats that have the taste of outdoor grill-

ing without the fuss, and pasties, the perfect, portable meal-in-one. Round out your tailgate party with crunchy vegetable salads and a chewy, tasty cornmeal roll.

Savor bright blue skies…the fragrance of food wafting through the air…the laughter and company of friends and family…and the satisfaction of enjoying these flavorful country classics.

TAILGATE TREATS: Clockwise from lower left—**Barbecued Chinese-Style Spareribs**, Mildred Danenhirsch, Bayville, New York (Pg. 78); **Cornmeal Rolls**, Marcella Swigert, Monroe City, Missouri (Pg. 78); **Harvest Popcorn**, Deanna House, Portage, Michigan (Pg. 78); **Hot Mulled Cider**, Maxine Zook, Middlebury, Indiana (Pg. 78); **Broccoli/Bacon/Raisin Salad**, Kammy Hilby, Manchester, Iowa (Pg. 79); **Crunchy Cabbage Salad**, Elaine Kremenak, Grants Pass, Oregon (Pg. 79); **Appetizer Meatballs**, Nona Yohe, Rich Hill, Missouri (Pg. 78); **Finnish Pasties**, Ruth Myers, Manchester, Michigan (Pg. 79).

P our the coffee…and pass the dessert! Every good tailgate party or picnic needs great-tasting portable treats —and the four cookie recipes featured here certainly fit the bill!

Baked to fill a large hand, the Mississippi Oatmeal Cookies and Mother's Oatmeal Cookies both bring country kitchens and grandma's cookie jar to mind.

Bar cookies are synonymous with potlucks and picnics, and these easy, cake-mix-based Pumpkin Cake bars and Caramel Turtle Brownies are two of the best-tasting take-alongs we've seen. Try them and see for yourself!

SWEET SUSTENANCE: Clockwise from lower left—**Pumpkin Cake Bars**, Martha Stroud, Clarksville, Texas (Pg. 80); **Mississippi Oatmeal Cookies**, Elizabeth McNeely, La Grange, Illinois (Pg. 79); **Mother's Old-Fashioned Oatmeal Cookies**, Arlene Larges, Hacienda Heights, California (Pg. 79); **Caramel Turtle Brownies**, Betsi Noser, Bowling Green, Kentucky (Pg. 80).

APPLE STREUSEL COFFEE CAKE
Loralee Hanes, Troy, Ontario

(PICTURED ON PAGE 68)

2-1/4 cups flour
3/4 cup sugar
3/4 cup butter
1/2 teaspoon baking powder
1/2 teaspoon baking soda
1 egg, beaten
3/4 cup buttermilk
1 can (20 ounces) apple pie filling
1/2 teaspoon grated lemon rind OR 1/2 teaspoon cinnamon, optional
1/3 cup raisins

Combine flour and sugar in large bowl. Cut in butter until mixture is crumbly; set 1/2 cup of the mixture aside. To remainder, add the baking powder and soda; set aside. Combine egg and buttermilk; add to dry ingredients, stirring just until moistened. Spread two-thirds of batter over bottom and part way up sides of greased 9-in. springform pan. Combine pie filling, flavorings (if desired) and raisins. Spoon over batter. Drop spoonfuls of remaining batter over the filling. Sprinkle with reserved crumb mixture. Bake at 350° for 1 hour.

APPLE SOUR CREAM BUNDT CAKE
Gayle West, Darwin, Minnesota

(PICTURED ON PAGE 68)

1/2 cup chopped walnuts
1 teaspoon cinnamon
1/2 cup sugar
1/2 cup butter
1 cup sugar
2 cups flour
1 cup dairy sour cream
2 eggs
1 teaspoon baking powder
1 teaspoon baking soda
1 teaspoon vanilla
1-1/2 cups finely chopped apples, *peeled*

CINNAMON CARAMEL GLAZE/SAUCE:
3/4 cup brown sugar
2 tablespoons butter
1/2 teaspoon cinnamon
1/3 cup *hot* evaporated milk

Combine nuts, cinnamon and sugar in small bowl; set aside. In large bowl, cream butter and sugar until light and fluffy. Add flour, sour cream, eggs, baking powder, soda and vanil-la; beat 3 minutes. Prepare the apples; set aside. Grease and lightly flour a bundt pan. Spread half of the batter in a pan; sprinkle with half of the nut mixture, then chopped apples. Sprinkle remaining nut mixture over apples then spread remaining batter over top. Bake at 350° for 60 minutes or until cake begins to pull away from sides of pan. Make glaze by putting all of ingredients in blender, covering and processing on HIGH until sugar is dissolved; set aside. Cool cake slightly on rack; remove from pan. Drizzle glaze/sauce over cake. **Yield:** 12-16 servings.

APPLE PIE BARS
Cindy Cyr, Fowler, Indiana

(PICTURED ON PAGE 68)

CRUST:
2 cups flour
1/2 cup sugar (optional)
1/2 teaspoon baking powder
1/2 teaspoon salt
1 cup butter
2 egg yolks, beaten

FILLING:
4 cups pared, cored and sliced apples (1/8 inch thick)
1/2 cup sugar
1/4 cup flour
1 teaspoon cinnamon
1/4 teaspoon nutmeg
2 egg whites, slightly beaten

Combine flour, sugar, baking powder and salt; cut in butter as for pie crust. Mix in egg yolks (mixture will be crumbly). Press *half* of the mixture in bottom of 15- x 10-in. jelly roll pan (may also use 13- x 9- x 2-in. pan). Set remaining half of the mixture aside. Combine all of filling ingredients *except egg whites;* arrange over bottom crust. Crumble remaining crust mixture over filling. Brush egg whites over all. Bake at 350° for 30 minutes (jelly roll pan) or 40 minutes (13- x 9- x 2-in. pan). Cool. Drizzle with thin confectioners' sugar glaze, if desired. **Yield:** 3-4 dozen bars.

APPLE ADVICE: To prevent any browning when working with a quantity of peeled apples, slice them into water with 1 tablespoon of fresh lemon juice added. •Don't forget this fruitful formula—2 to 3 medium-sized apples make about 1 lb. • For moist and colorful poultry stuffing, add 1 diced, unpeeled apple to your favorite stuffing mix.

APPLE BREAD PUDDING
Martha Doyle, Kalispell, Montana

(PICTURED ON PAGE 68)

4 cups soft bread crumbs, crusts trimmed
1 cup diced apples, *peeled*
2 cups scalded milk
2 tablespoons butter, melted
3 eggs
1/3 cup honey OR 1/2 cup sugar
1 teaspoon vanilla
1 teaspoon cinnamon
1/4 teaspoon nutmeg
1/4 teaspoon cloves
1 teaspoon grated lemon rind

Mix bread (white, whole wheat or combination) with apples; set aside. Combine milk, butter, eggs, honey/sugar, vanilla, cinnamon, nutmeg, cloves and rind in blender or with hand mixer. Pour over bread/apple mixture. Spoon into a buttered 2-qt. casserole or individual ramekins, as shown. Set dish in a larger pan of hot water; bake at 350° for 1 hour or until knife inserted in center comes out clean. Serve warm with whipped cream or ice cream. **Yield:** 6 servings. **Diabetic Exchanges:** One serving equals 1 fruit, 1 bread, 3/4 milk, 2 fats; also 281 calories, 271 mg sodium, 149 mg cholesterol, 38 gm carbohydrate, 9 gm protein, 11 gm fat.

APPLE/SAUSAGE/SWEET POTATO CASSEROLE
Irene Gerdes, Red Wing, Minnesota

(PICTURED ON PAGE 69)

1 pound seasoned *lean* bulk pork sausage
1/4 cup water
1 can (23 ounces) sweet potatoes, drained
1/4 to 1/2 cup brown sugar
1/4 cup butter
3 medium apples, red cooking variety

Form sausage into patties; brown in a skillet. Drain. Place patties in bottom of 2-qt. casserole. Add water. Layer thick slices of sweet potatoes over sausage. Sprinkle with sugar; dot with half of the butter. Top with sliced, unpeeled apple rings, cut 1/2 in. thick. Dot with the remaining butter. Cover; bake 30 minutes at 350°. Uncover; bake for 15 more minutes. **Yield:** 4 servings.

APPLE STREUSEL MUFFINS
June Isaac, Abbotsford, British Columbia

(PICTURED ON PAGE 69)

2 cups flour
1 cup sugar
1 tablespoon baking powder
1-1/4 teaspoons cinnamon
1/2 teaspoon salt
1/2 teaspoon baking soda
2 large eggs, beaten
1 cup dairy sour cream
1/4 cup butter, melted
1 cup finely diced apples, *unpeeled*

STREUSEL TOPPING:
1/4 cup granulated sugar
3 tablespoons flour
1/4 teaspoon cinnamon
2 tablespoons butter

In large bowl, stir together flour, sugar, baking powder, cinnamon, salt and baking soda; set aside. In small bowl, beat eggs, sour cream and butter. Add all at once to dry ingredients along with apples. Stir just until moistened. Fill well-greased muffin tins two-thirds full. Combine topping ingredients; sprinkle on. Bake at 400° for 20-25 minutes. **Yield:** 18 muffins.

PRIZE-WINNING APPLE PIE
Ruth Unruh, Newton, Kansas

(PICTURED ON PAGE 69)

CRUST:
2 cups flour
1 teaspoon salt
1/2 teaspoon baking powder
2/3 cup butter-flavored shortening
1 tablespoon vegetable oil
4 to 5 tablespoons milk

FILLING:
1 cup sugar
4 tablespoons cornstarch
3/8 teaspoon nutmeg
3/8 teaspoon cinnamon
Dash salt
4-1/2 cups thinly sliced, pared tart apples (I use Jonathans)
1 tablespoon water
2 tablespoons butter

Measure flour, salt and baking powder into large bowl; mix well. Cut in shortening until mixture resembles small peas. Sprinkle in oil then milk, 1 tablespoon at a time, tossing with fork after each addition. When it's thoroughly mixed, press dough firmly together with hands as you would a snowball. Divide dough into two balls. Roll out each piece on a lightly floured pastry cloth. Put bottom crust into 9-in. pie pan; set aside. Prepare filling by stirring together the sugar, cornstarch, nutmeg, cinnamon and salt; mix with apples and water. Turn into pastry-lined pan; dot with butter. Cover with top crust; seal and flute. Slit steam vents in top crust. Cover edge with aluminum foil to prevent over-browning. Bake at 425° for 25 minutes. Remove foil last 15 minutes of baking.

TASTY TEA: For Apple-Mint Tea, combine 4 cups apple juice with 1-1/2 cups of chopped fresh spearmint. Microwave or cook on stovetop until mixture boils. Let steep 30 minutes; strain.

FRESH APPLE CAKE
Joan Baskin, Black Creek, British Columbia

(PICTURED ON PAGE 69)

1-3/4 cups coarsely chopped apples, *peeled*
1 cup sugar
1-1/3 cups flour
1 teaspoon baking soda
1/2 teaspoon salt
1 teaspoon cinnamon
1/2 teaspoon nutmeg
1/2 teaspoon allspice
1/2 cup vegetable oil
1 egg
1/2 cup raisins
1/2 cup chopped walnuts

Combine prepared apples and sugar in large mixing bowl; let stand 10 minutes. Sift flour; add soda, salt, cinnamon, nutmeg and allspice; set aside. Blend oil and egg into apple/sugar mixture. Add dry ingredients, stirring just until blended. Fold in the raisins and walnuts. Spread evenly in a greased 8-in. square pan. Bake at 350° for 50-55 minutes. Cool 10 minutes. Sprinkle with confectioners' sugar. **Yield:** 6-8 servings.

APPLE/CRANBERRY CRISP
Candie Takacs, West Carrollton, Ohio

(PICTURED ON PAGE 70)

3 cups chopped apples, *unpeeled*
2 cups raw cranberries
3/4 to 1 cup granulated sugar

TOPPING:
1-1/2 cups old-fashioned OR quick-cooking oats
1/2 cup brown sugar, packed
1/3 cup flour
1/3 cup chopped pecans
1/2 cup butter, melted

Combine apples, cranberries and sugar in 8-in. square baking dish or 2-qt. casserole; mix thoroughly to blend; set aside. Combine topping ingredients until crumbly; spread evenly over fruit layer. Bake at 350° for 1 hour or until the fruit is fork-tender. Serve warm with ice cream or whipped cream. **Yield:** 8 servings.

✓ FRESH APPLE SALAD
Becky Druetzler, Indianapolis, Indiana

(PICTURED ON PAGE 70)

8 cups chopped, tart red apples, *unpeeled*
1 can (20 ounces) pineapple chunks, drained—*reserve juice*
2 cups seedless green grapes
1 to 2 teaspoons poppy seeds
1-1/2 cups toasted pecans

DRESSING:
Reserved pineapple juice
1/4 cup butter
1/4 cup sugar
1 tablespoon lemon juice
2 tablespoons cornstarch
2 tablespoons water
1 cup mayonnaise OR 1/2 cup reduced-calorie mayonnaise and 1/2 cup plain yogurt

Make dressing first by combining the reserved pineapple juice, butter, sugar and lemon juice in a small saucepan. Heat to boiling. Combine the cornstarch and water to make a smooth paste; add to the hot mixture; cook until thick and smooth. *Chill completely* before stirring in mayonnaise/yogurt. Combine apples, pineapple chunks, grapes and

---

APPLE SNACKS: Spread crunchy peanut butter on apple wedges for a quick and healthy snack. • Top a toasted English muffin with applesauce and grated sharp cheese or cinnamon. • Make mini carameled apples by dipping quartered apples on toothpicks into melted caramel (1 package of caramels melted in a double boiler).

poppy seeds in large glass bowl. Add chilled dressing; refrigerate until time to serve. Stir in pecans right before serving for maximum crunchiness. **Yield:** 16 servings. **Diabetic Exchanges:** One serving equals 1-1/2 fruits, 3 fats; also, 206 calories, 86 mg sodium, 12 mg cholesterol, 22 gm carbohydrate, 2 gm protein, 14 gm fat.

APPLE, RAISIN, WALNUT CAKE
Pollie Malone, Ames, Iowa

(PICTURED ON PAGE 70)

    3 eggs
    1 cup vegetable oil
    2 cups sugar
    1 teaspoon vanilla
    4 cups grated apples, *unpeeled*
    2 cups sifted flour
    1 teaspoon baking soda
  1/2 teaspoon salt
    1 teaspoon cloves
    1 teaspoon cinnamon
  1/2 cup raisins
  3/4 cup chopped walnuts
NON-SWEET FROSTING:
    5 tablespoons flour
    1 cup milk
    1 cup butter
    1 cup confectioners' sugar
    1 teaspoon vanilla
  1/2 cup broken walnuts

Beat eggs and oil together in a mixing bowl until foamy; add sugar and vanilla and continue to beat. Add apples, beating slightly; set aside. Sift together flour, soda, salt, cinnamon and cloves; add raisins and walnuts to flour mixture. Add flour mixture to egg mixture; beat slightly. Bake at 350° in greased 13- x 9- x 2-in. pan. Check for doneness after 25 minutes. To make frosting, mix milk and flour in saucepan; heat over medium heat until thick. Chill thoroughly over ice water. Beat in large mixer bowl with butter, sugar and vanilla until mixture is light and fluffy, about 5 minutes (like mashed potatoes). Spread on cooled cake; sprinkle with nuts. **Yield:** 12 servings.

APPLE SAUSAGE BREAKFAST RING
Cherie Sechrist, Red Lion, Pennsylvania

(PICTURED ON PAGE 70)

    2 pounds *lean* bulk pork sausage
    2 large eggs, slightly beaten
1-1/2 cups crushed Ritz crackers

    1 cup grated apple, *peeled*
  1/2 cup minced onion
  1/4 cup milk

Line a 2-1/2-qt. ring mold with plastic wrap *or* wax paper. Combine all ingredients; mix well and press firmly into mold. Chill several hours or overnight. Unmold, removing plastic/paper, onto a baking sheet *with raised edges*. Bake at 350° for 1 hour. Transfer onto a serving platter; fill center of ring with scrambled eggs. **Yield:** 8 servings.

FALL APPLE DIP
Loretta Harmon, Utica, Illinois

    1 package (8 ounces) cream cheese, room temperature
  3/4 cup brown sugar
    1 teaspoon vanilla
    1 cup salted peanuts, chopped
Golden Delicious apples
Orange juice

Blend together all ingredients *except last two*. Wash and slice apples; dip in orange juice. Drain. Arrange in concentric circles on pretty plate and place the dip in center in a bowl. Sprinkle additional chopped peanuts on top of dip. Refrigerate leftovers.

FALL APPLE DIP (Light Version)

    1 package (8 ounces) *lite* cream cheese, room temperature
    1 carton (8 ounces) vanilla yogurt
  1/3 cup brown sugar
  1/2 teaspoon vanilla
    1 to 2 cups unsalted peanuts, chopped
Granny Smith apples
Orange juice

(Directions same as above.)

APPLE PITA PIE
Sharon Loh, Trumbull, Connecticut

    1 apple, peeled, cored and quartered
    1 medium-sized pita (white or whole wheat)
    1 teaspoon butter
    1 teaspoon to 1 tablespoon

    sugar OR 1 packet artificial sweetener
Cinnamon to taste
Whipped cream or nondairy whipped topping

Stuff pita bread with apple quarters. Add butter, sugar/substitute and cinnamon. Wrap in foil; place on cookie sheet. Bake at 350° for 20 minutes. Remove foil. (**Microwave Version:** Wrap in paper towel and MW on HIGH for 5 minutes.)

SPICED APPLE TWISTS
Amy Kraemer, Glencoe, Minnesota

  1/4 cup orange juice (water can be substituted)
    1 can crescent rolls
    2 large tart, firm apples, peeled and cored
    2 tablespoons butter, melted
  1/2 teaspoon cinnamon
  1/3 cup sugar

Pour orange juice in bottom of buttered 9-in. square baking pan. Unroll crescent roll dough; separate into eight triangles. Cut each lengthwise to make 16 triangles. Cut each apple into eight pieces. Place an apple slice at wide end of each strip; roll up. Arrange in pan. Drizzle butter over tops, then sprinkle with combined cinnamon and sugar mixture. Bake at 400° for 30-35 minutes until golden in color. Serve warm or cold. **Yield:** 16 twists.

APPLE AND BLACK WALNUT CREAM
Teresa Wester, Palmyra, Missouri

    1 cup plain yogurt
    1 tablespoon lemon juice
1-1/2 tablespoons honey
    4 medium-size tart eating apples, peeled and cored
    1 cup black walnuts, chopped

Combine the yogurt, lemon juice and honey, mixing well to blend. Shred apples into yogurt mixture, stirring after each addition to prevent discoloration. Stir in nuts and serve immediately.

AMISH SOUR CREAM APPLE PIE

Clara Yoder, Millersburg, Ohio

1 cup dairy sour cream
1 egg
3/4 cup sugar
2 tablespoons flour
1/4 teaspoon salt
1 teaspoon vanilla
2-1/2 cups diced, peeled apples
1 unbaked 9-inch pie shell

CRUMB TOPPING:
1/2 cup brown sugar
1/3 cup flour
1/4 cup butter
1 teaspoon cinnamon

Beat cream and egg together; add flour, sugar, salt and vanilla. Mix until smooth. Stir in apples. Bake at 400° for 25 minutes; remove pie from oven. Spread with crumb topping that has been mixed until crumbly. Bake 20 minutes more. **Yield: 8 servings.**

HOT MULLED CIDER

Maxine Zook, Middlebury, Indiana

(PICTURED ON PAGE 72)

2 quarts fresh apple cider
1 teaspoon grated orange rind, no white membrane
1/2 teaspoon whole allspice
1/4 teaspoon mace
1/8 teaspoon salt, if desired
1/2 teaspoon ground coriander
1 teaspoon whole cloves
1 tablespoon cinnamon candy (red hots)

Bring all ingredients to boil in large kettle; reduce heat and simmer for 30 minutes. Serve hot with orange slices or whole cinnamon sticks. **Yield: 8 one-cup servings.**

BARBECUED CHINESE-STYLE SPARERIBS

Mildred Danenhirsch, Bayville, New York

(PICTURED ON PAGE 72)

2 pounds pork spareribs
MARINADE:
2 cloves garlic, minced
3 tablespoons soy sauce
1 tablespoon cooking sherry
3 to 5 tablespoons hoisin sauce*
1 tablespoon honey

1 tablespoon chicken broth
1 tablespoon vegetable oil

Have butcher cut between each rib, halfway down, for easier eating of ribs. Trim off excess fat. Mix all marinade ingredients together. *Hoisin sauce, a reddish/brown, spicy, sweet sauce is available in the Oriental section of most supermarkets. Place ribs in a large container and pour marinade mixture over ribs. Marinate, in refrigerator, about 3 hours, turning each hour. Roast ribs on a foil-covered rack in large pan at 400° for 45 minutes. Baste occasionally with any leftover marinade. **Yield: 4 servings.**

CORNMEAL ROLLS

Marcella Swigert, Monroe City, Missouri

(PICTURED ON PAGE 72)

1/3 cup cornmeal, stone ground preferred
1/2 cup sugar
2 teaspoons salt
1/2 cup shortening
2 cups milk
1 package active dry yeast
1/4 cup warm water (110-115°)
2 beaten eggs
4 cups flour or more as needed
Melted butter
Cornmeal

Cook cornmeal, sugar, salt, shortening and milk in medium saucepan until thick (like cooked cereal). Cool to lukewarm. Add yeast which has been dissolved in lukewarm water, then eggs. Beat thoroughly. Add flour to form soft dough. Knead well on lightly floured surface. Place in bowl; cover; let rise. Punch down. Roll out to 1 in. thickness; cut with 2-1/2 in. biscuit cutter. Brush with melted butter; dust with cornmeal. Place on greased cookie sheet; cover; let rise. Bake at 375° for 15 minutes. (Dough will keep in refrigerator for several days.) **Yield: 18 rolls.**

> **QUICK 'N' EASY APPETIZERS:**
> *Combine catsup and brown sugar to taste; add cocktail sausages or slices of hot dogs. Heat and serve in a slow cooker or a fondue pot. • Spread 1 8-oz. package of cream cheese on a large plate. Top with cocktail sauce; sprinkle with drained canned or frozen shrimp. Serve with crackers.*

HARVEST POPCORN

Deanna House, Portage, Michigan

(PICTURED ON PAGE 72)

2 quarts freshly popped popcorn, *unsalted*
2 cans (1-3/4 ounces each) shoestring potatoes, 3 cups
1 cup salted mixed nuts
1/4 cup butter *or* margarine, melted
1 teaspoon dried dill weed
1 teaspoon Worcestershire sauce
1/2 teaspoon lemon/pepper seasoning
1/4 teaspoon garlic powder
1/4 teaspoon onion powder

In large roasting pan or aluminum foil turkey roasting pan, combine popcorn, shoestring potatoes and nuts. Set aside. In small bowl, combine melted butter, dill weed. Worcestershire sauce, lemon/pepper seasoning, garlic powder and onion powder. Pour over popcorn mixture, stirring until evenly coated. Bake in preheated 325° oven, 8-10 minutes, stirring mixture once. Cool. Store in airtight containers. **Yield: 2-1/2 quarts.**

APPETIZER MEATBALLS

Nona Yohe, Rich Hill, Missouri

(PICTURED ON PAGE 73)

2 pounds lean ground beef
1 pound bulk pork sausage
1 can (5 ounces) evaporated milk
2 cups old-fashioned oats
1/2 teaspoon ground pepper
2 teaspoons chili powder
1/2 teaspoon garlic powder
2 to 3 teaspoons salt
2 eggs
1/2 cup chopped onions

SAUCE
(If you like sauce, double this recipe):
2 cups catsup
1-1/2 cups brown sugar
1 teaspoon liquid smoke
1/2 teaspoon garlic powder
1/2 cup chopped onions

Mix all meatball ingredients together; shape into small 1-in. diameter balls. Place in baking pan in single layer. Combine sauce ingredients and pour over meatballs. Bake at 350° for 1 hour. **Yield: 9 dozen meatballs.**

BROCCOLI/BACON/ RAISIN SALAD

Kammy Hilby, Manchester, Iowa

(PICTURED ON PAGE 73)

1 bunch fresh broccoli, washed, drained, broken into flowerettes
1/2 cup chopped red onion
1 cup celery, chopped
1 pound bacon, fried crisp, drained and crumbled
1/2 cup hulled sunflower seeds
1/2 cup raisins

DRESSING:
3/4 cup mayonnaise
1/4 cup sugar
2 tablespoons vinegar

Combine salad ingredients together in large mixing bowl. Set aside. Combine dressing ingredients together thoroughly. Pour dressing over salad ingredients; stir to blend. Serve chilled. Refrigerate leftovers. **Yield:** 12 servings.

FINNISH PASTIES

Ruth Myers, Manchester, Michigan

(PICTURED ON PAGE 73)

CRUST:
3 cups flour
1 teaspoon salt
1 cup lard
1 egg, beaten
1 teaspoon vinegar
5 tablespoons cold water

FILLING:
2 cups potatoes, peeled and diced
3/4 to 1 cup carrots, peeled and diced
3/4 pound ground beef (can use part pork sausage)
1/4 cup onions, diced 1/2-in.
1-1/4 cups rutabaga, peeled and diced
2 tablespoons Worcestershire sauce
Salt
Pepper
1/4 teaspoon poultry seasoning
Butter
Egg glaze

Cut together flour, salt and lard in mixing bowl. Add and blend the beaten egg, vinegar and water. Chill dough while mixing filling. Combine filling ingredients. Roll out pie crust into six to seven (6-inch) rounds. Place approximately 1/2 cup of fill-ing on one-half of pie crust. Put a pat of butter on filling; fold other half of pie crust over filling and pinch edges together. Repeat with other pasties. Brush with egg glaze made of beaten whole egg and 1 tablespoon of water. Make steam vents with fork in decorative starburst pattern. Bake at 375° for 15 minutes; reduce heat to 350° and bake for 60 minutes more. **Yield:** 6-7 pasties.

CRUNCHY CABBAGE SALAD

Elaine Kremenak, Grants Pass, Oregon

(PICTURED ON PAGE 73)

1 head green cabbage
1 package Oriental chicken-flavored noodle mix (reserve chicken flavor packet for dressing)
4 green onions, sliced thinly

DRESSING:
1/2 cup vegetable oil
1 tablespoon sugar
1/2 teaspoon black pepper
1 package chicken flavoring from noodle mix
2 tablespoons sesame seeds, toasted
1/2 cup sliced almonds, toasted

Shred or finely chop cabbage. Add onions and noodles (crushed with your hands). Mix well; cover; set in refrigerator for 1 hour, no longer. Mix dressing ingredients thoroughly. Refrigerate until serving time. Toast seeds and almonds in oven at 350° for about 7 minutes. Toss dressing with cabbage mixture; add toasted seeds and almonds. **Yield:** 10 servings.

MOTHER'S OLD-FASHIONED OATMEAL COOKIES

Arlene Larges, Hacienda Heights, California

(PICTURED ON PAGE 74)

1 cup margarine, softened
1 cup light brown sugar
1 cup granulated sugar
2 unbeaten eggs, room temperature
2 teaspoons vanilla extract
1-1/4 cups sifted all-purpose flour
1 teaspoon salt
1 teaspoon baking soda
1 teaspoon cinnamon
1/2 teaspoon cloves
1/2 teaspoon allspice
3 cups old-fashioned oats
3/4 cup chopped pecans
Confectioners' sugar

In large bowl, blend margarine, sugars, eggs and vanilla; beat until fluffy. Combine flour, salt, baking soda, cinnamon, cloves and allspice. Add to creamed mixture; mix to blend. Stir in oats and pecans. Drop by teaspoonsful onto cookie sheet lined with parchment paper. Flatten with floured fork to 2-in. diameter (will spread to 4 in. when baked). Bake at 350° for 12-15 minutes. Cool on cookie sheet; remove to cooling rack. Sift confectioners' sugar over tops. **Yield:** 3 dozen large cookies.

MISSISSIPPI OATMEAL COOKIES

Elizabeth McNeely, La Grange, Illinois

(PICTURED ON PAGE 74)

1 egg, beaten
1-3/4 cups sugar
3/4 cup shortening (one-half butter; one-half vegetable shortening)
1/2 cup milk
1/4 teaspoon ginger
1/4 teaspoon allspice
1/4 teaspoon cloves
2-1/2 cups flour
1-1/2 teaspoons baking soda
1-1/2 teaspoons salt
2 cups old-fashioned oats
1 cup raisins
1 egg white, beaten
Sugar for tops of cookies

Beat egg in mixing bowl; add sugar, shortening, milk and spices; blend. Stir in flour, baking soda and salt. Add oats and raisins; mix well. Chill dough overnight. Next morning, shape dough into golf-ball size. Flatten balls on ungreased cookie sheets to 2-in. diameter with fork dipped in beaten egg white and sprinkle with bit of sugar. Brush each with beaten egg white and bake at 350° until golden brown, about 15 minutes for a chewy cookie. Let cookies cool on cookie sheet for a few minutes; remove to wire rack to complete cooling. **Yield:** 2 dozen large cookies.

CARAMEL TURTLE BROWNIES

Betsi Noser, Bowling Green, Kentucky

(PICTURED ON PAGE 74)
1 bag (14 ounces) caramels
1 can (5 ounces) evaporated milk *or* 2/3 cup, *divided*
1 devil's food chocolate cake mix
1/2 to 1 cup chopped nuts
6 tablespoons butter *or* margarine, melted
1 package (6 ounces) semisweet chocolate chips
Pecan halves for garnish

Unwrap caramels (there are enough for the cook to sneak a few) and place in saucepan with *2 tablespoons evaporated milk*. Set aside. In a mixing bowl, combine the remaining evaporated milk, dry cake mix, melted butter/margarine and the nuts. Stir until well-blended. Spread half of this mixture in a greased 13- x 9- x 2-in. baking pan. (Mixture will form thin layer in pan.) Bake at 350° for 10 minutes only. Meanwhile, melt the caramels over medium to low heat; stir constantly. Be careful not to burn. Remove brownies from oven; sprinkle with chocolate chips and drizzle melted caramels over the top. Cover evenly. Drop remaining cake mixture by teaspoons over all. Return pan to oven for 20 minutes more. *Do not overbake.* Cut while warm but do not remove from pan until completely cooled. They must "set up". Garnish with toasted pecan halves, if desired. **Yield:** 24 brownies.

PUMPKIN CAKE BARS

Martha Sue Stroud, Clarksville, Texas

(PICTURED ON PAGE 74)
4 eggs, well beaten
2 cups cooked pumpkin *or* 1 can (1 pound)
1-1/2 cups sugar
1/4 teaspoon salt
1 teaspoon ginger
1 teaspoon cinnamon
1/2 teaspoon cloves
1 yellow cake mix
1/2 cup butter, melted
1 cup chopped pecans

Mix eggs, pumpkin, sugar, salt, ginger, cinnamon and cloves together; pour into a 13- x 9- x 2-in. pan. Sprinkle dry cake mix on top. Drizzle melted butter over mix; spread chopped nuts over all. Bake at 325° for 1 hour and 20 minutes. (Cover with foil loosely to keep from browning too soon for the first half of cooking time.) Cut into squares; serve topped with whipped cream. **Yield:** 24 bars.

HOMEMADE PEANUT BUTTER CUPS

Collette Frederick, Lisbon, Iowa

1 cup semisweet chocolate chips
2/3 cup peanut butter
2 tablespoons butter
1/3 to 1/2 cup peanut butter
Small paper liners (bonbon)

Mix chocolate, 2/3 cup peanut butter and butter together in glass measure and MW on HIGH for 1-1/2 to 2 minutes. Pour 1/2 of chocolate mixture in bottom of paper liners. Melt remaining peanut butter by microwaving on HIGH for 1 minute. Spoon melted peanut butter on top of chocolate layer in liners and cover with remaining chocolate mixture. Cool; store covered. **Yield:** about 1 dozen.

MICROWAVE MAPLE SYRUP

Kathleen Davison, Braddyville, Iowa

1 cup white sugar
1 cup brown sugar
1 cup white corn syrup
1 cup water
1 teaspoon maple flavoring

Combine all ingredients in 2-qt. glass measure. MW on HIGH until mixture boils. Boil 5-7 minutes, stirring twice. Store in clean syrup bottle and reheat in microwave (removing metal cap).

DEL RIO CHILI CON QUESO

Roselle Coates, Big Spring, Texas

1 medium onion, finely chopped
1 tablespoon butter
1 4-ounce can chopped green chilies
1 8-ounce can jalapeno relish
1 8-ounce can taco sauce
2 pounds Velveeta cheese, cubed
3 tablespoons milk

Saute onion in butter in 1-qt. glass measure. Add chilies, relish and taco sauce to onion/butter. Stir. MW cheese and milk in large mixing bowl on HIGH until cheese is melted. Stir at 1-minute intervals. Add onion/pepper mixture. Serve warm with corn chips.

SPICY SHRIMP

Roselle Coates, Big Spring, Texas

1 10-ounce package frozen medium-size shrimp, defrosted, rinsed
1/4 cup melted butter (may substitute 1/4 cup white wine)
1/2 teaspoon garlic powder
1/2 teaspoon parsley flakes
1/8 teaspoon black pepper
1/8 teaspoon salt
1/8 teaspoon tarragon
1 small bay leaf
Dash red pepper flakes OR pimento

Combine all ingredients in 2-qt. casserole. Cover with wax paper. MW on HIGH for 3-1/2 to 6 minutes or until shrimp are opaque, stirring every 2 minutes. Let stand 3-5 minutes. Serve hot in chafing dish.

SNACK OYSTER CRACKERS

David Harter, Allendale, Michigan

1 pound box oyster crackers
1 cup vegetable oil
1 package reduced calorie Ranch-style dressing mix
1-1/4 teaspoon dill weed
1 teaspoon lemon pepper seasoning

Place crackers in 6-quart bowl; set aside. Combine oil, dressing mix, dill weed and lemon pepper; whip well. Pour over crackers; mix thoroughly. Spread on cookie sheet; bake at 250° for 1 hours; stirring three times. Store in airtight container. Delicious as snack or great with soups.

APPETIZER ANGLE: Spread cream cheese combined with dill weed on party rye bread slices. Top each with a cucumber slice; sprinkle lightly with dill weed.

Best Cook

Dedication, discipline, imagination and a sense of humor are the attributes that make Arla Ewy, Riceville, Iowa, the "Best Cook in the Country", says her son Gary Severson of Everson, Washington.

"Mom's always cooked equally well for two or 21 people, and never complained about adding an extra place at the table," he wrote.

"She's been responsible for feeding not only her immediate family, but also the extended family of seasonal farm workers. Everyone was always well fed, no matter how Mom felt.

"Cooking 365 days a year may be exhausting, but it didn't show in her meals, or in her positive attitude as she served them. Mom's piping hot corn bread and encouraging words gave us the energy to finish the hardest farm chores.

"She always wears a smile and likes a lot of laughter at the table. And thanks to her organizational skills, Mom is able to prepare a huge dinner when there hardly seems time to boil water. She's always modest, too, never expecting compliments for her scrumptious fried chicken or delicious desserts."

HEATH BARS

2 cups brown sugar, packed
2 cups all-purpose flour
1/2 cup butter
1 egg
1 cup milk
1 teaspoon baking soda
3/4 teaspoon salt
1 teaspoon vanilla
1/2 cup nuts, chopped
6 English toffee bars
  (1.2 ounces each)

Combine sugar, flour and butter as for pie crust; reserve 1 cup. To remaining crumb mixture, add egg, milk, soda, salt and vanilla, mixing well to combine. Spread into 13-in. x 9-in. x 2-in. baking pan. Sprinkle reserved cup of crumbs over top evenly, then chopped nuts. Crush toffee bars and sprinkle over all. Bake at 350° for 35 minutes. Cool in pan. Cut. **Yield:** 48 bars.

FRESH STRAWBERRY PIE

1 cup sugar
1/4 cup cornstarch
1/4 teaspoon salt
1-1/2 cups water
1 package (3 ounces)
  strawberry gelatin
  dessert mix
About 1 quart fresh strawberries
1 baked 9-inch pie shell

Combine in saucepan sugar, cornstarch, salt and water; cook, stirring constantly, until clear. Add gelatin mix; stir to blend. Cool mixture to room temperature. Arrange washed, drained fresh strawberries in shell; pour sauce over berries. Chill. Serve with whipped cream, if desired. **Yield:** 8 servings.

ROSY RED RHUBARB CAKE

CAKE:
1/4 cup butter
2 cups sifted all-purpose flour
2-1/2 teaspoons baking powder
1/4 teaspoon salt
1/4 cup brown sugar, packed
1 egg, slightly beaten
3/4 cup milk
6 cups thinly sliced,
  washed rhubarb
1 package (3 ounces)
  strawberry gelatin
  dessert mix

TOPPING:
6 tablespoons butter
1-1/2 cups sugar
1/2 cup flour

Cut butter into flour, baking powder, salt and brown sugar as for pie crust. Add egg and milk; mix well. Spread into a 13-in. x 9-in. x 2-in. baking pan. (Mixture will be moist.) Top with rhubarb. Sprinkle powdered gelatin mix over rhubarb. Combine topping ingredients like pie crust; sprinkle over top. Bake at 350° for 60 minutes. Serve warm or cool. **Yield:** 12 servings.

BANANA DESSERT

CRUST:
1/2 cup butter
1 cup flour

FILLING:
1 package (8 ounces)
  cream cheese
1 cup confectioners' sugar
1 carton (12 ounces) nondairy
  whipped topping, *divided*
4 large bananas
2 packages (3 ounces *each*)
  banana-flavored instant
  pudding mix
3 cups chilled milk

Combine butter and flour as for pie crust; press into bottom of 13-in. x 9-in. x 2-in. baking pan. Bake at 350° for 8 minutes. Cool. Prepare filling by combining cream cheese, confectioners' sugar and *half* of whipped topping; spread over cooled crust. Slice bananas over cream layer. Combine pudding mix with milk; beat with electric mixer on slow speed for 2 minutes. Pour over top of bananas. Spread remaining half of whipped topping over all. Chill until serving time; refrigerate leftovers. **Yield:** 16-20 servings.

MICROWAVE TIPS: To speed up rice cereal/marshmallow bars, butter a large bowl; put marshmallows and butter in bowl; microwave on HIGH for 2-3 minutes. • Toast coconut in the microwave by spreading 1/2 cup coconut in a glass pie plate. Microwave on HIGH for 3-4 minutes. Stir every 30 seconds after first 2 minutes. • For squeaky, better-flavored cheese curds, microwave on HIGH for 30 seconds.

Country Inns

♥

Vista Verde Guest & Ski Touring Ranch
Box 465
Steamboat Springs, Colorado 80477
303/879-3858

Directions: Vista Verde Ranch is located near Clark, about 25 miles north of Steamboat Springs. From U.S. 40, take Colorado 129 north through Clark to Seedhouse Road. East 5 miles to ranch entrance. Ranch provides pickup at Steamboat Springs upon request.

Owners: Frank and Winton Brophy.

Schedule: Open year-round.

Rates and Accommodations: Five log cabins, each with one to three bedrooms, with fireplaces and kitchenettes. Summer rates: $1,050 per person, Sunday to Sunday stay. Daily rate, $150/day/person. Rate includes transfer from airport, horseback riding, use of the spa, three meals, evening entertainment and a day of whitewater rafting. Winter rates: $60/day/person, with a 3-night minimum stay, including use of ski trails, spa, sleigh rides and snowshoeing. Children's rates also available. Hours and rates are subject to change. Please call or write.

A dude ranch during the summer and a picturesque cross-country ski resort during the winter, the Vista Verde Ranch always has a complement of hungry guests—and the hearty, wholesome food it serves reflects that.

Days begin with filling ranch breakfasts, which may include strawberry juice, vegetable quiche, hash brown potatoes and cream cheese coffee cake (recipe below). Lunch could include broccoli salad, cheese soup, garlic corn bread and cookies—either at the lodge or in a picnic sack lunch. After a day riding the range or skiing the trails, savory appetizers such as Mushroom Croustades hold guests over until dinnertime.

Guests are served at colorful, casual tables in the main lodge, enjoying such dinner menus as watercress salad with fresh mushrooms and homemade dressing, smoky-flavored roast beef, grits, broccoli casserole and homemade onion rolls, topped off by a flavorful coconut almond torte for dessert.

Here's a sampling of the inn's recipes:

CHEESE-FILLED COFFEE CAKE

    1 package (1 tablespoon) dry yeast
1/4 cup lukewarm water
    1 teaspoon sugar
    1 egg, lightly beaten
    2 cups flour, sifted
1/4 teaspoon salt
3/4 cup butter *or* margarine
    2 packages (8 ounces each) cream cheese, room temperature
    1 cup sugar
    1 teaspoon fresh lemon juice
Powdered sugar

Mix yeast, water and 1 teaspoon sugar. Let stand 10 minutes. Add egg. Cut butter or margarine into flour and salt; mix well. Add yeast mixture. Roll dough on waxed paper into 12- x 15-in. rectangle. Make filling by combining cream cheese, lemon juice and 1 cup sugar. Spread filling on dough to within 1 in. of edges. Fold each long edge toward middle, making sure edges overlap. Fold ends up about 1-1/2 in. Flip onto baking sheet so folds are down. Bake immediately at 375° for about 30 minutes. Cool and sprinkle with powdered sugar.

MUSHROOM CROUSTADES

48 very thin slices of bread
    4 tablespoons soft margarine, room temperature
    4 tablespoons butter
    3 tablespoons finely chopped green onion
1/2 pound mushrooms, finely chopped
    2 tablespoons flour
    1 cup heavy cream
    1 tablespoon minced parsley
1-1/2 teaspoons minced chives
1/2 teaspoon fresh lemon juice
1/2 teaspoon salt
1/8 teaspoon cayenne pepper

Cut 2-1/2-in. circles from bread. Lightly spread margarine on each side and press into 1-3/4-in. muffin tins. Bake 10 minutes at 350°. Cool. (Store in airtight container or freeze.) In 10-in. skillet, melt butter; add green onion and cook over moderate heat for 4 minutes. Add the mushrooms; cook 10-15 minutes. Remove from heat; sprinkle flour over mixture while stirring. Return skillet to heat. Pour in heavy cream; stir and heat to boiling. When thickened, simmer and cook 1 minute. Remove from heat. Add parsley, chives, lemon juice, salt and cayenne. Cool. Refrigerate or freeze until use. Fill shells; bake at 350° for 10 minutes. Cool 5 minutes; serve. **Yield:** 48 appetizers.

GOLDEN HOT MUSTARD SAUCE

In medium bowl, mix:
    3 cans (2 ounces each) dry mustard
1/2 teaspoon ground black pepper
1/4 teaspoon ground white pepper
1/4 teaspoon ground red pepper

To this add:
1/2 cup cold water

Beat until smooth. Add:
    2 cups of sugar
1-1/2 cups cider vinegar
    1 teaspoon salt

Pour mixture into blender, beat briefly and add:
    3 beaten eggs
1/8 pound of softened butter

Beat all until smooth, then pour into saucepan and boil 3-5 minutes, stirring constantly. **Yield:** Approximately 4-1/2 cups sauce.

MORNING MICROWAVING: To separate 1 pound of cold bacon slices, microwave on HIGH for 15-20 seconds. Let stand 3-5 minutes.
• Scramble eggs with cottage cheese for a moist, high-protein dish. Use 1/3 cup of cottage cheese for each two eggs. Microwave on HIGH for 1-1/2 minutes; stir. Microwave 1-1/2 minutes more. • For perfectly buttered/sweetened pancakes, microwave butter and syrup together on HIGH 1-2 minutes. Pour over pancakes.

Best Cook

Generous as well as talented, Jim Boilini of Monroe County, Florida relishes sharing the fruits of his labor with family, friends and neighbors. This "Best Cook in the Country" regularly hosts fish fries for 15 and pasta parties heaped high with delicious Italian dishes, says his neighbor, Karen Beal, who nominated him.

"Jim is a great cook!" she wrote. "He knows a lot about our local cuisine, including Key Lime Pie and seafood dishes galore. After he won our Island Jubilee Cooking Contest 2 years in a row with his conch chowder, the judges ended up making him chairman and host!"

Later, Jim shared the reasons why he became such an enthusiastic cook.

"I was raised in an Italian household, and I credit my mamma with my interest in cooking. My fondest memories are of sitting at the dinner table with relatives, enjoying the most delicious food imaginable—and of Mamma's eyes sparkling with satisfaction as she watched us eat.

"Now I, too, get my biggest thrill not so much from eating what I cook, but in watching other people enjoying it. Life is good, and eating well adds to its pleasure."

GRILLED FLANK STEAK

2-3 pounds flank steak
1 garlic clove, split in half
3/4 cup soy sauce, divided
2 teaspoons dry mustard
2 teaspoons brown sugar

Rub garlic into steak on both sides. Let stand 10 minutes. Moisten surface well with soy sauce; pat in dry mustard and brown sugar. (Use a fork to work it into the meat.) Put meat in large zip-lock bag; add enough soy sauce to partially cover meat. Marinate 2-3 hours, turning bag over periodically. Let the steak stand at room temperature for 30 minutes before grilling on a very hot grill. Sear on each side, then cook 3-4 minutes per side for medium. Slice diagonally against the grain. Serve with rice or pasta. **Yield: 4-6 servings.**

BROILED TOMATOES

6 firm, ripe tomatoes
6 teaspoons olive oil
3 teaspoons basil
1 teaspoon oregano
3 teaspoons bread crumbs
1 small clove garlic, minced
4 tablespoons Assiago *or* Parmesan cheese, grated

Slice tops off tomatoes; squeeze out seeds. Salt insides and turn upside down on paper towel. Combine all other ingredients other than cheese and fill tomato cavity with the mixture. Top with grated cheese. Bake at 325° for 10 minutes, then brown under broiler. **Yield: 6 servings.**

SHRIMP SCAMPI

1 pound cleaned, deveined, uncooked shrimp (size 16-20 or 20-25 are best)
1/4 cup butter and olive oil (total)
1 teaspoon white pepper
3 cloves garlic, chopped
1 tablespoon chopped onion
Juice of 1 lemon
1/4 cup water
1 tablespoon flour
1 cup sliced mushrooms
1 cup green onions, coarsely chopped
1 tablespoon parsley

Heat butter and olive oil. Saute garlic and onion until clear. Turn off and set aside for 10 minutes. Sprinkle white pepper over shrimp; reheat skillet. Saute shrimp and mushrooms until shrimp are opaque. Juice the lemon into shrimp. Mix flour and water and stir in until desired thickness. Serve over rice, garnished with green onions and parsley. **Yield: 4 servings.**

MAMMA'S ANTIPASTO

VEGETABLE MIXTURE:
2 stalks celery, thinly sliced
2 medium carrots, thinly sliced
1/2 teaspoon salt
1/4 teaspoon pepper
1 small bay leaf, crumbled

MARINADE:
1/2 cup catsup
1 can (2 ounces) anchovies
1 clove garlic, minced
1/2 cup olive oil
1/4 cup wine vinegar
1 green pepper, sliced

1 can (7-1/2 ounces) pitted whole black olives
1 jar pickled onions
1 can (16 ounces) water-packed tuna
1 large dill pickle, sliced
1 jar (2 ounces) pimientos
1 can (4-1/2 ounces) whole mushrooms

Combine vegetable mixture; heat briefly in a small amount of water until vegetables are cooked but still crunchy. Drain and set aside. In a 3-qt. kettle, combine marinade ingredients; boil about a minute. Add vegetable mixture and remaining ingredients. Bring to a boil and cool. Let it marinate for a day or two, stirring occasionally. Serve with crackers or toasted Italian bread. **Yield: 2-1/2 qts.**

BARBECUED SHRIMP AND SCALLOPS: Marinate 1 pound cleaned and deveined jumbo shrimp and 1 pound well-washed scallops in a marinade of 1/3 cup soy sauce, 1/3 cup olive oil, 1/3 sherry or wine vinegar, 1/2 teaspoon onion powder and 1/4 teaspoon ground ginger for 1 hour. Alternate seafood with wedges from 2-3 green peppers and one large onion. Grill over hot fire for no longer than 10 minutes, rotating skewers and basting with marinade mixture.

Here's fancy festive food that's fit for a season of entertainment and feasting!

Press your prettiest tablecloth, polish your silver and celebrate in style with the taste treats pictured below. Choose from an array of appetizers and desserts, some "fussy" to fix, others fast and easy.

No matter which recipe you choose, there's one thing you'll find —every one is delicious!

FANCY FARE! Clockwise from lower left—**Hot Cheddar Stuffed Mushrooms**, Joan Ward, Brownsburg, Indiana (Pg. 91); **Pineapple Fruit Plate with Dip**, Virginia Quelch, Las Cruces, New Mexico (Pg. 91); **Shrimp Appetizer Platter**, Tammy Norberg, Marquette, Manitoba (Pg. 91); **Southwest Cheesecake**, Lori Walton, Stuttgart, Arkansas (Pg. 92); **Mother Ertelt's Meatballs**, Earlene Ertelt, Woodburn, Oregon (Pg. 91); **Stuffed Phyllo Pastries**, Anita Moffett, Rewey, Wisconsin (Pg. 92); **Salmon Pate**, Gudrun Braker, Burnett, Wisconsin (Pg. 92); **Fudge Swirl Toffee Pie**, Jan Hill, Sacramento, California, (Pg. 91).

♥

Party food from A to D—from appealing appetizers to delicious dessert, that is!

These favorites set a fancy, festive mood from the moment guests set eyes on them. The appealing swirl of the Tortilla Pinwheels... the medley of colors in the Bread Pot Fondue...the smooth white shape of the Russian Creme, contrasting with fresh garnish...and the mouth-wateringly rich look of the Chocolate/Whipping Cream Torte make any holiday buffet table look extra special.

The only thing better than their looks? Their taste, of course.

Try one or more at your next festive occasion...and savor the season!

FESTIVE FAVORITES! Clockwise from top—**Chocolate/Whipping Cream Torte**, Rita Futral, Ocean Springs, Mississippi (Pg. 92); **Appetizer Tortilla Pinwheels**, Pat Waymire, Yellow Springs, Ohio (Pg. 93); **Russian Creme**, Jeanne Bloedom, Fond du Lac, Wisconsin (Pg. 93); **Bread Pot Fondue**, Katie Dreibelbis, Santa Clara, California (Pg. 93).

Recipes from Terry Fulchen, Marco Island, Florida.

meals in MINUTES

TIME FLIES when suppertime comes for a hungry family. That's why you'll appreciate this tasty, nutritious meal, which is ready in less than 30 minutes.

There are many different cuts of economical, no-waste turkey available today—cuts that can be prepared in many different ways. This Turkey Meatball Tetrazzini uses ground turkey in an imaginative, quick-cooking dish.

Begin this 30-minute menu by mixing the quick-to-bake cranberry cake from a prepared biscuit mix. Pre-heat the oven when you come in, mix up the cake, pop it in, and let it bake while you eat the rest of the meal.

Prepare the turkey meatballs and get the other ingredients for the stir-fry organized. Then, as you brown the meatballs, heat the water to cook the pasta. Once the meatballs are browned, the rest of the dish goes together quickly.

A quick, colorful salad rounds out the meal. To speed salad making, keep your greens washed and crisped in the refrigerator, and use a commercially prepared dressing.

TURKEY MEATBALLS TETRAZZINI

      1 slice whole wheat bread
  3/4 pound uncooked ground
        turkey
      1 clove garlic, pressed
  1/2 teaspoon dried basil leaves
  1/2 teaspoon salt
Pepper (to taste)
      1 teaspoon butter
      1 onion, peeled and sliced
  1/4 pound fresh mushrooms,
        cleaned and quartered
1-1/2 cups milk
      2 tablespoons flour
  1/4 cup Parmesan cheese
Chopped fresh parsley
Angel hair pasta *or* other favorite
        pasta (cooked according to
        package directions)

Crumble the bread into a medium bowl. Blend in ground turkey, garlic, basil, salt and pepper. Form turkey mixture into 1-in. meatballs. Melt butter in large skillet. Saute meatballs on all sides, loosening them carefully before turning. Stir in onion and mushrooms; saute until golden. Whisk flour into milk, whipping until smooth; add to skillet. Cook, stirring constantly, until thickened. Fold in the cheese. Place cooked, drained pasta on serving plate. Spoon tetrazzini into center. Sprinkle with parsley and additional cheese, if desired. **Yield:** 4 servings.

CAULIFLOWER/PEPPER SALAD

      1 head Boston lettuce, washed
        and crisped
      1 small head cauliflower
      1 green *or* red pepper
  1/3 cup commercial oil and
        vinegar dressing

Line a salad bowl with lettuce. Wash cauliflower and green/red pepper. Cut cauliflower into 1/4-in. slices. Remove seeds from pepper and slice. Place cauliflower and pepper in center of lettuce. Pour 1/3 cup dressing over all. Serve immediately. **Yield:** 4 servings.

FRESH CRANBERRY CAKE

      1 cup fresh cranberries
1-1/2 cups biscuit mix
  1/4 cup sugar
      1 egg, slightly beaten
  1/3 cup milk
      2 tablespoons sugar

Wash and drain cranberries; remove any stems. Set aside. In medium bowl, combine biscuit mix, 1/4 cup sugar, egg and milk until just blended. Spoon into a greased and floured 8-in. round or star-shaped pan. Toss cranberries with 2 tablespoons sugar; spoon evenly over cake batter. Bake at 375° for 20-30 minutes or until golden brown and firm when gently pressed. Cool cake on rack. Remove from pan and cut into wedges. Serve with a scoop of vanilla ice cream, if desired.

P
ull up a chair and
join us—it's time for holiday feasting with family and friends! Our
table is decked out with dishes that
provide refreshing new twists on
traditional favorites.

Pique your appetite with spicy。

Mississippi-style baked shrimp of the fresh flavors and festive colors of pickled mushrooms. Serve up a crisply brown roasted duckling, but instead of the usual bread stuffing, try our pleasant brown rice/pecan variation.

Accompany it with acorn squash, baked with an intriguing and fla- vorful filling of hot Italian sausage and maple syrup. And save room to savor the tart, richly smooth taste contrast of a colorful and un- usual salad of avocado and pink grapefruit. Round out the feast with colorful, apple-studded red cabbage, a cranberry salad liberally laced with orange and flavorful, feather- weight sourdough rolls.

HOLIDAY FEAST: Clockwise from lower left—**Avocado/Grapefruit Sal- ad**, Caroline Weiler, Sarasota, Florida (Pg. 94); (on same plate) **Sourdough Butterflake Refrigerator Rolls**, Kalli Deschamps, Missoula, Montana (Pg. 94); **Pickled Mushrooms**, Mavis Di- ment, Marcus, Iowa (Pg. 93); **Renais- sance Red Cabbage**, Angela Biggin, La Grange Park, Illinois (Pg. 93); **Duck with Brown Rice Stuffing**, Nancy Brissey, Auburn, Washington (Pg. 94); **Baked Squash with Sausage**, Donie Kaup, Albion, Nebraska (Pg. 94); **Fresh Cranberry Salad**, Cathy Burke, Oneida, Tennessee (Pg. 94); **Biloxi-Style Ap- petizer Shrimp**, Diane Hixon, Nice- ville, Florida (Pg. 94).

Leave room for dessert—especially when the sideboard boasts these spectacular treats!

'Tis the season for special desserts—and that's what you're tasting when you sink your fork into a rich and smooth classic cheesecake …or a light, chocolate and almond-studded torte with a whipped cream filling. Spoon up some buttery fresh cranberry topping or a cool, coffee-flavored ice cream pie. Try two!

DESSERT DELIGHTS: Clockwise from lower left—**Mississippi Mud Pie**, Sara Carley, Temple, New Hampshire (Pg. 33); **Ultimate Cheesecake**, Cathy Burke, Oneida, Tennessee (Pg. 95); **Chocolate Torte**, Rose Johnson, Virginia, Minnesota (Pg. 92); **Cranberry Topping**, Kristi Twohig, Fond du Lac, Wisconsin (Pg. 95).

PINEAPPLE FRUIT PLATE WITH DIP

Virginia Quelch, Las Cruces, New Mexico

(PICTURED ON PAGE 84)

1 ripe fresh pineapple
1 medium-size watermelon
2 large cantaloupes *or* 1 cantaloupe and 1 honeydew melon
Red seedless grapes

FRUIT DIP:
1/2 cup sugar
4 teaspoons cornstarch
1/2 teaspoon salt
1 cup *unsweetened* pineapple juice
3 tablespoons lemon juice
2 eggs, beaten
2 packages (3 ounces each) cream cheese, softened

Cut pineapple into quarters, starting at top; *do not remove leaves.* Remove hard center core with sharp knife. Separate remaining pineapple from shell and slice into bite-size pieces. Scoop melon balls from melons; chill. Wash and chill grapes. To make dip, combine sugar, cornstarch and salt in saucepan; blend in fruit juices. Cook, stirring constantly until clear, about 5-8 minutes. Slowly pour cooked mixture into beaten eggs, beating briskly. Return mixture to saucepan; cook over low heat, stirring constantly 3-5 minutes or until mixture thickens slightly. Cool 5 minutes. Beat softened cream cheese in small bowl, then blend into cooled mixture. Chill thoroughly. To serve, place crushed ice on a large glass cake plate with outer lip. Set a pretty glass bowl, about 1-1/2-cup size, in center of plate. Tuck down into ice and fill with dip. Place 4 pineapple quarters at right angles on plate, with leaves pointing out. Fill spaces between pineapple with melon balls and grapes. Refrigerate leftovers. **Yield:** 32 servings. **Diabetic Exchanges:** One serving equals 2 fruits, 1/2 fat; also, 151 calories, 28 gm sodium, 18 gm cholesterol, 32 gm carbohydrate, 3 gm protein, 3 gm fat.

HOT CHEDDAR STUFFED MUSHROOMS

Joan Ward, Brownsburg, Indiana

(PICTURED ON PAGE 84)

1 pound large fresh mushrooms (about 16 mushrooms)
6 tablespoons butter
1 cup chopped onions
1 cup soft bread crumbs
1 cup shredded cheddar cheese
1/2 cup chopped walnuts
1/4 cup chopped parsley
1/2 teaspoon salt
1/4 teaspoon black pepper

Rinse mushrooms and pat dry. Remove stems, chop and set aside. In large skillet, melt butter. Brush mushroom caps with melted butter; place on lightly buttered shallow baking pan or broiler pan. To remaining butter in skillet, add onions and reserved mushroom stems. Saute 2 minutes. Add crumbs, cheese, nuts, parsley, salt and pepper; stir lightly. Spoon into mushroom caps, piling high. Bake at 350° until hot, about 20 minutes. Serve hot. **Yield:** 16 stuffed mushrooms. **Diabetic Exchanges:** One mushroom equals 1 vegetable, 2 fat; also, 107 calories, 188 mg sodium, 20 mg cholesterol, 4 gm carbohydrate, 4 gm protein, 9 gm fat.

SHRIMP APPETIZER PLATTER

Tammy Norberg, Marquette, Manitoba

(PICTURED ON PAGE 84)

1 package (8 ounces) cream cheese, softened
1/2 cup dairy sour cream
1/4 cup mayonnaise
2 cans (4-1/4 ounces *each*) broken shrimp, drained and rinsed
1 cup seafood sauce
2 cups shredded mozzarella cheese
1 green pepper, chopped
3 green onions, chopped
1 large tomato, diced

Combine the cream cheese, sour cream and mayonnaise; spread over 12-in. pizza pan. Scatter shrimp on cheese layer; cover with seafood sauce. Then layer on the cheese, green pepper, onion and tomato. Cover and chill until serving time. Serve with assorted crackers.

FUDGE SWIRL TOFFEE PIE

Jan Hill, Sacramento, California

(PICTURED ON PAGE 84)

1/2 cup semisweet chocolate chips
2 tablespoons milk
1 package (8 ounces) cream cheese, softened
1 jar (7 ounces) marshmallow creme
1/2 cup brown sugar
1 cup chopped almonds, *toasted*
1 container (8 ounces) whipped topping with *real* cream, thawed, *divided*
1 chocolate wafer crumb crust (9 inches), homemade or purchased

Melt chips with milk in small saucepan over a low heat, stirring until smooth. Cool; set aside. Combine cream cheese, marshmallow creme and the sugar, mixing at medium speed until well-blended. Fold in almonds and 2-1/2 cups whipped topping. Combine the chocolate mixture and *remaining* whipped topping. Spread half of the marshmallow creme mixture over crust; cover with all of chocolate mixture and carefully top with remaining half of marshmallow creme mixture. Cut through layers several times with a knife to swirl. Freeze. **Yield:** 6-8 servings.

MOTHER ERTELT'S MEATBALLS

Earlene Ertelt, Woodburn, Oregon

(PICTURED ON PAGE 85)

MEATBALLS:
1-1/2 pounds *lean* ground beef
1 egg, beaten
1 envelope *dry* onion soup mix
3 tabelspoons water
2 tablespoons Worcestershire sauce
Stuffing—pitted black olives, green stuffed olives, cocktail onions or pineapple tidbits

SAUCE:
1 bottle (12 ounces) chili sauce
1 jar (18 ounces) grape jelly
1/4 cup lemon juice
3 tablespoons horseradish

Combine all meatball ingredients; mix well. Using about 1 tablespoon of meatball mixture, form balls by covering each olive, cocktail onion and pineapple tidbit. Arrange meatballs in shallow baking dish; bake at 375° for 20 minutes. Combine sauce ingredients; pour over meatballs. Return to oven for 15 minutes or until the sauce thickens slightly. Serve from a chafing dish or crock pot with wooden picks for easy spearing. **Yield:** About 30 meatballs.

SOUTHWEST CHEESECAKE
Lori Walton, Stuttgart, Arkansas

〰〰〰〰〰〰〰〰〰〰〰〰〰〰〰〰〰〰〰

(PICTURED ON PAGE 85)

16 ounces cream cheese, softened
2 cups sharp shredded cheddar cheese
2 cups dairy sour cream, *divided*
1-1/2 packets taco seasoning
3 eggs, room temperature
1 can (4 ounces) green chilies, chopped and drained

2/3 cup salsa
Tortilla chips

Combine cheeses; beat until fluffy. Stir in *1 cup* of sour cream and taco seasoning. Beat in eggs, one at a time. Fold in chilies. Pour into 9-in. springform pan. Bake at 350° for 35-40 minutes or until center is just firm. Remove from oven; cool 10 minutes. Spoon remaining sour cream over top of cake; return to oven for 5 minutes. Cool completely on wire rack. Refrigerate, covered, overnight. Remove from pan; place on serving plate. Top with salsa. Serve with tortilla chips. **Yield: 50 servings.**

〰〰〰〰〰〰〰〰〰 ♥ 〰〰〰〰〰〰〰〰〰

✓ SALMON PATE
Gudrun Braker, Burnett, Wisconsin

〰〰〰〰〰〰〰〰〰〰〰〰〰〰〰〰〰〰〰

(PICTURED ON PAGE 85)

1 can (15-1/2 ounces) salmon
1 package (3 ounces) cream cheese, room temperature
1 tablespoon fresh lemon juice
1 teaspoon prepared horseradish
1 teaspoon grated onion
1/4 teaspoon salt
1/8 teaspoon pepper
1/8 teaspoon liquid smoke

Garnishes—sliced almonds, stuffed green olive, celery stalk, parsley

Drain, debone and flake salmon. Mix together with all other ingredients except garnishes. On a pretty platter, mold mixture into a fish shape. Arrange almonds to resemble scales. Use slice of olive for eye, thin strips of celery for the tail. Garnish with parsley. Chill until serving time. Serve with buttery crackers. Refrigerate leftovers. **Yield: 16 servings.** (each about 2 tablespoons). **Diabetic Exchanges:** One serving

equals 1/2 meat, 1 fat; also, 69 calories, 197 mg sodium, 16 mg cholesterol, .5 gm carbohydrate, 6 gm protein, 5 gm fat.

〰〰〰〰〰〰〰〰〰 ♥ 〰〰〰〰〰〰〰〰〰

STUFFED PHYLLO PASTRIES
Anita Moffett, Rewey, Wisconsin

〰〰〰〰〰〰〰〰〰〰〰〰〰〰〰〰〰〰〰

(PICTURED ON PAGE 85)

FILLING:
1 package (10 ounces) frozen chopped spinach, thawed
1 pound feta cheese, crumbled
3 ounces grated Parmesan cheese
2 eggs, beaten
1 teaspoon nutmeg
1/2 teaspoon pepper

1 pound frozen phyllo dough, thawed 24 hours in refrigerator
1 to 1-1/2 cups unsalted butter, melted

To make filling, press spinach in fine strainer to remove all excess moisture; combine with cheeses, eggs, nutmeg and pepper. Set aside. To assemble pastries, have at ready melted butter, a pastry brush, knife, a clean, slightly damp towel, filling, baking sheet and large work surface. Open box of dough; carefully unfold sheets. Pull off 2 sheets; place together on work surface and brush lightly with butter. Pull off another sheet. Place directly over others; brush again with butter. Repeat until you have layered 5 sheets. Cover unused dough with damp towel. Cut prepared layers in half vertically, then cut halves into 6 strips vertically (see illustrations). Place 1-1/2 teaspoons of filling at the top of each strip. Fold each strip into triangles (as you would fold a flag), starting at bottom near filling. Repeat with additional layers of phyllo dough until the filling is gone. Place pastries on ungreased cookie sheet; brush with butter. Bake at 400° until golden brown, about 10-15 minutes. (Uncooked pastries can be frozen for later use. Frozen pastries can go directly into oven, but baking time must be increased.) **Yield: About 60 pastries.**

CHOCOLATE/WHIPPING CREAM TORTE
Rita Futral, Ocean Springs, Mississippi

〰〰〰〰〰〰〰〰〰〰〰〰〰〰〰〰〰〰〰

(PICTURED ON PAGE 86)

CAKE:
1/2 cup butter
3 squares (3 ounces) unsweetened chocolate
1-1/2 cups whipping cream
4 eggs, well beaten
1 teaspoon vanilla
1-1/2 cups sugar
2 cups flour
2 teaspoons baking powder
1/2 teaspoon salt

FILLING:
1 cup whipping cream
1 package (8 ounces) cream cheese, softened
1 cup confectioners' sugar, sifted
1 teaspoon vanilla

ICING:
1/4 cup butter
2 squares (2 ounces) unsweetened chocolate
1/2 cup whipping cream
1 teaspoon vanilla
3 cups confectioners' sugar sifted

To make the cake, melt the butter with chocolate over low heat. Cool; set aside. Beat cream until soft peaks form. Reduce mixer speed to low; add cooled chocolate mixture, beaten eggs and vanilla to whipped cream until just mixed. Sift together sugar, flour, baking powder and salt. With mixer on low speed, add dry ingredients to creamed mixture until just mixed. Pour into three greased and floured 8-in. or 9-in. round pans. Bake at 350° for 20-25 minutes or until done. Cool in pans for 5 minutes; turn onto cooling racks. Cool completely; wrap tightly and refrigerate. To make filling, whip cream until soft peaks form. Set aside. Beat the cream cheese until smooth and creamy; add sugar and vanilla, mixing well. Add whipped cream to cream cheese mixture and beat until smooth. Set aside. Split chilled cake layers in half. Divide filling and spread between cake layers. Chill while preparing icing. To make icing, melt butter with chocolate; cool. Add whipping cream and vanilla to chocolate mixture; blend well. Add sugar; beat until of spreading consistency. Frost cake with the icing; refrigerate until serving time. Garnish with fresh strawberries dipped in melted chocolate. **Yield: 22 servings.**

RUSSIAN CREME

Jeanne Bloedorn, Fond du Lac, Wisconsin

(PICTURED ON PAGE 86)

CREME:
- 1 cup sugar
- 2-1/4 cups water
- 2 envelopes unflavored gelatin
- 1-1/2 cups dairy sour cream
- 1-1/2 teaspoons vanilla
- 1-1/2 cups heavy cream, whipped

TOPPING:
- 1 package (10 ounces) frozen raspberries
- 1 package (4-3/4 ounces) raspberry-flavored Danish Dessert *or* pie glaze

Dissolve sugar and gelatin in water over low heat. Remove from stove; stir in the sour cream and vanilla until smooth. Chill the mix until slightly thickened (like unbeaten egg whites). Fold in whipped cream with wire whisk until well blended. Pour into greased 6-cup ring mold; chill until set. To make topping, drain raspberries, reserving juice. Prepare dessert mix, following package directions for pudding, using raspberry juice as part of liquid. Chill topping; fold in raspberries. To serve, turn molded cream onto glass serving plate (at least 1 in. larger than mold). Put the raspberry topping in small bowl in center of mold. Guests serve themselves by taking a slice of creme pudding and spooning topping over it. **Yield:** 10-12 servings.

APPETIZER TORTILLA PINWHEELS

Pat Waymire, Yellow Springs, Ohio

(PICTURED ON PAGE 86)

FILLING:
- 8 ounces dairy sour cream
- 1 package (8 ounces) cream cheese, softened
- 1 can (4 ounces) diced green chilies, well drained
- 1 can (4 ounces) chopped black olives, well drained
- 1 cup grated cheddar cheese
- 1/2 cup chopped green onion
- Garlic powder to taste
- Seasoned salt to taste
- 5 (10-inch) flour tortillas
- Fresh parsley for garnish
- Salsa

Mix all of the filling ingredients together thoroughly. Divide the filling and spread evenly over the tortillas; roll up tortillas. Cover tightly with plastic wrap, twisting ends; refrigerate for several hours. Unwrap; cut in slices 1/2 in. to 3/4 in. thick. (An electric knife works best.) Discard ends. Lay pinwheels flat on glass serving plate; garnish with parsley. Leave space in center of plate for small bowl of salsa if desired. **Yield:** About 50 pinwheels.

RENAISSANCE RED CABBAGE

Angela Biggin, La Grange Park, Illinois

(PICTURED ON PAGE 88)

- 1 head red cabbage, about 5 pounds
- 1 cup dry red wine, burgundy or zinfandel *or* unsweetened apple juice
- 3 tablespoons white *or* apple cider vinegar
- 1/4 teaspoon salt
- 1/8 teaspoon ground pepper
- 1/8 teaspoon ground cloves
- 2 teaspoons ground cinnamon
- 2 whole bay leaves
- 3 tablespoons sugar
- 5 tablespoons whole *or* jellied cranberry sauce
- 2 cooking apples, peeled and cubed 1/2-inch
- 1/2 cup sweetened applesauce

Shred cabbage in food processor or by hand. Combine with wine and vinegar in large kettle. Cover; bring to boil. Reduce heat to low; cook about 5 minutes. Add salt, pepper, cloves, cinnamon, bay leaves, sugar, cranberry sauce and apples. Cook about 20 minutes. Add applesauce. Remove bay leaves before serving. Serve with roast pork or duckling. **Yield:** 16-20 servings.

BREAD POT FONDUE

Katie Dreibelbis, Santa Clara, California

(PICTURED ON PAGE 86)

- 1 firm, round loaf of bread (1-1/2 pounds, 8 to 10 inches in diameter)

FILLING:
- 2 cups (8 ounces) sharp shredded cheddar cheese
- 2 packages (3 ounces *each*) cream cheese, softened
- 1-1/2 cups dairy sour cream
- 1 cup (5 ounces) diced cooked ham
- 1/2 cup chopped green onion
- 1 can (4 ounces) whole green chilies, drained and chopped
- 1 teaspoon Worcestershire sauce
- 2 tablespoons vegetable oil
- 1 tablespoon butter, melted
- Assorted raw vegetables for dipping—broccoli, pepper strips, cauliflower, celery, carrot sticks, mushroom caps

Slice off top of bread loaf, reserving top. Carefully hollow out inside of loaf with small paring knife, leaving 1/2-in. shell. Cut the removed bread into 1-in. cubes (about 4 cups); reserve. To make filling, combine the cheeses and sour cream in bowl; stir in ham, green onion, chilies and Worcestershire sauce. Spoon filling into hollowed loaf; replace top. Wrap loaf tightly with several layers of heavy-duty aluminum foil; set on cookie sheet. Bake at 350° for 1 hour and 10 minutes or until filling is heated through. Meanwhile, stir together bread cubes, oil and melted butter. Arrange on a separate cookie sheet. Bake at 350°, turning occasionally, for 10 to 15 minutes or until golden brown. Remove filled loaf from oven; unwrap and transfer to platter. Remove top from bread; stir filling and serve with toasted cubes and vegetables as dippers.

PICKLED MUSHROOMS

Mavis Diment, Marcus, Iowa

(PICTURED ON PAGE 88)

- 2 pounds fresh mushrooms, cleaned

DRESSING:
- 1/2 cup olive oil
- 1/4 cup lemon juice
- 1/4 cup water
- 1 teaspoon minced garlic
- 3/4 teaspoon salt
- 1/2 teaspoon pepper
- 1/3 cup chopped fresh parsley
- 1/4 cup diced red bell pepper

Place mushrooms in pretty glass bowl; set aside. Mix oil, juice, water, garlic, salt and pepper in saucepan and bring to a boil. Pour over mushrooms. Cover; refrigerate for at least 2 hours. Add the parsley and pepper, stirring to blend. **Yield:** 10 appetizer servings.

AVOCADO/GRAPEFRUIT SALAD WITH POPPY SEED DRESSING
Caroline Weiler, Sarasota, Florida

(PICTURED ON PAGE 88)

2 ripe avocados, peeled, pitted and sliced lengthwise into 1/4-in. slices
2 large red grapefruit, peeled and sectioned with white membranes removed
Boston lettuce leaves, washed and chilled

POPPY SEED DRESSING:
1/3 cup sugar
1 teaspoon dry mustard
5 tablespoons vinegar
1 teaspoon salt
1 cup vegetable oil
1-1/2 teaspoons grated onion, drained on paper towel
2-1/2 teaspoons poppy seeds

Arrange several slices of avocado and grapefruit on a bed of lettuce, alternating slices for color; chill. Make dressing by mixing sugar, mustard, vinegar and salt. Slowly add oil, beating vigorously between additions (dressing will be very thick). Stir in grated onion and poppy seeds. Spoon on salads and serve immediately. **Yield:** 8 servings.

DUCK WITH BROWN RICE STUFFING
Nancy Brissey, Auburn, Washington

(PICTURED ON PAGE 88)

STUFFING:
1 cup brown rice
2 cups chicken stock
1 cup green onions, sliced 1/8-in. with tops
1 cup diced celery
1/2 cup butter
5 to 6 ounces (1-1/2 cups) sliced fresh mushrooms
1 teaspoon salt
1 cup pecan pieces, 1/4-in. pieces
1 duckling, about 5 pounds, rinsed and dried with paper towel

Prepare stuffing by cooking rice in chicken stock in covered heavy saucepan until liquid is absorbed, about 40 minutes. While rice is cooking, saute green onions and celery in skillet in butter until vegetables are tender. Add mushrooms and saute about 5 minutes. Stir in salt, cooked rice and pecan pieces. Stuff duck.

Preheat oven to 450°. Place duck on rack in roasting pan; *immediately* lower temperature to 350° and roast, uncovered, until tender, allowing about 25 minutes per pound. Allow to rest for 10 minutes before carving. Serve with stuffing. **Yield:** 4 servings.

BAKED SQUASH WITH SAUSAGE
Donie Kaup, Albion, Nebraska

(PICTURED ON PAGE 88)

2 small acorn squash
4 tablespoons pure maple syrup
2 tablespoons butter
8 ounces bulk hot Italian sausage

Cut squash in half; clean seeds from cavity. Put a fourth of maple syrup, butter and sausage in each cavity. Place squash on baking sheet. Bake at 350° for 30-40 minutes or until fork tender. **Yield:** 4 servings.

SOURDOUGH BUTTERFLAKE REFRIGERATOR ROLLS
Kalli Deschamps, Missoula, Montana

(PICTURED ON PAGE 89)

SOURDOUGH STARTER RECIPE:
NOTE: Starter must be made 2-3 days in advance.
2 cups all-purpose flour
1 teaspoon salt
3 tablespoons sugar
1 tablespoon dry yeast
2 cups lukewarm water

Stir together flour, salt, sugar and yeast with wooden spoon in large mixing bowl; gradually add lukewarm water. Stir until mixture resembles a smooth paste. Cover with towel or cheesecloth; set in warm (85°) place. Stir mixture several times a day. Ready in 2-3 days. Store in heavy plastic container with air hole for gases to escape.

SOURDOUGH REFRIGERATOR ROLLS:
NOTE: Dough must "rest" overnight.
2 packages dry yeast
1/3 cup warm water (110°)
1 cup sourdough starter
1/2 cup vegetable oil
3 eggs well beaten
1 cup warm water
1/2 cup sugar
1 teaspoon salt
5-1/2 to 6-1/2 cups all-purpose flour

1/4 cup melted butter

Soften yeast in 1/3 cup warm water; set aside. In a large mixing bowl, combine the starter, oil, eggs, 1 cup of warm water, sugar, salt and 2 cups flour. Stir vigorously for 1 minute. Stir in softened yeast and enough flour to make dough that pulls away from sides of bowl. Cover with cloth; set in warm, draft-free place to let rise until doubled. Punch down; cover with plastic wrap. Refrigerate overnight. Three hours before baking, roll out dough on lightly floured surface to 1/4-in. to 1/2-in. thick rectangle, about 7 in. wide and 26 in. long. Brush with butter. Starting with long side, roll up jelly-roll style. Cut into 1-in. slices. Place in greased muffin pans, cut side down. Cover with cloth. Let rise until double, about 2-1/2 hours. Bake at 400° for 12-15 minutes until golden brown. **Yield:** 2-1/2 dozen rolls.

FRESH CRANBERRY SALAD
Cathy Burke, Oneida, Tennessee

(PICTURED ON PAGE 89)

1 package (12 ounces) fresh cranberries, washed and sorted
1-1/2 cups sugar
3 cups boiling water
3 packages (3 ounces *each*) orange gelatin dessert
2 cans (11 ounces *each*) mandarin oranges, drained and cut in small pieces
1 cup chopped nuts, walnuts *or* pecans
1 can (8 ounces) crushed pineapple, undrained

Grind cranberries in food grinder *or* food processor; stir in the sugar to blend. Set aside. Dissolve gelatin dessert in water; cool until mixture begins to thicken. Add to cranberry mixture. Add oranges, nuts and pineapple. Stir well; pour into lightly oiled 8-cup mold. Chill overnight. Unmold and serve on plate of crisp greens. **Yield:** 16 servings.

BILOXI-STYLE APPETIZER SHRIMP
Diane Hixon, Niceville, Florida

(PICTURED ON PAGE 89)

1 bag shrimp and crab boil

2 cans (12 ounces *each*) beer
or water
1 tablespoon Tabasco sauce
1 tablespoon Worcestershire
sauce
1 teaspoon salt
1/2 teaspoon garlic powder
Pepper to taste
3 tablespoons fresh lemon *or*
lime juice
5 pounds fresh medium-sized
shrimp, shelled and deveined
1 cup unsalted butter, melted

Bring spice bag to boil in beer/water in large saucepan. Add the Tabasco and Worcestershire sauces, salt, garlic powder, pepper and lemon/lime juice. Simmer for 10 minutes to blend flavors. Arrange shrimp in an oven-proof casserole. Pour liquid over them. Pour melted butter over all. Bake at 350° for 15 minutes, stirring twice. **Yield:** 20 appetizer servings.

THE ULTIMATE CHEESECAKE
Cathy Burke, Oneida, Tennessee

(PICTURED ON PAGE 90)
CRUST:
1 cup all-purpose flour
1/4 cup sugar
1 teaspoon grated lemon peel
1/2 teaspoon vanilla
1 egg yolk
1/4 cup butter, softened
FILLING:
5 packages (8 ounces *each*)
cream cheese, softened
1-1/4 cups sugar
3 tablespoons all-purpose flour
1/4 teaspoon vanilla
5 eggs
2 egg yolks
1/4 cup whipping cream
2 teaspoons grated lemon peel
1-1/2 teaspoons grated orange peel
GLAZE:
2 tablespoons sugar
4 teaspoons cornstarch
2 cans (8 ounces *each*) crushed
pineapple, undrained
2 teaspoons lemon juice
1 perfect strawberry for garnish

Make crust by mixing all ingredients

until blended. Pat half of the crust mixture on bottom of greased 9-in. springform pan (sides of pan should be *well-greased* as well). Bake at 400° until golden brown, about 6-8 minutes; cool. Press the rest of dough to sides of pan; set aside. Make filling by mixing cheese, sugar, flour and vanilla at high speed. Add eggs and the egg yolks one at a time, beating well after each addition. Beat in the cream; stir in the grated peels. Pour into assembled springform pan; bake at 500° for 10 minutes. Lower oven temperature to 250°; bake for 1 hour. Remove to rack to cool for at least 2 hours. Refrigerate cheesecake. Make glaze by mixing the sugar and cornstarch together; add pineapple and lemon juice. Bring to boil over medium heat. Cook for 1 minute until thick. Cool; top the cooled cheesecake with glaze. Chill for at least 3 hours (overnight is best). Remove sides of pan; top cheesecake with single strawberry, if desired.

CRANBERRY TOPPING
Kristi Twohig, Fond du Lac, Wisconsin

(PICTURED ON PAGE 90)
1/2 cup butter
1 cup white *or* brown sugar
1 package (12 ounces) whole
cranberries, washed and
sorted
1/2 cup orange liqueur *or* orange
juice concentrate
1/2 cup whipping cream, optional

Combine butter, sugar, cranberries and orange liqueur/concentrate. Bring to boil over medium heat, stirring constantly. Reduce heat; simmer until berries pop. Remove from heat; stir in cream, if desired. Serve warm or at room temperature over pound cake, cheesecake or ice cream. Makes a nice Christmas gift—be sure to include instructions to store under refrigeration. **Yield:** 4 cups.

CHOCOLATE TORTE
Rose M. Johnson, Virginia, Minnesota

(PICTURED ON PAGE 90)
TORTE:
8 eggs, separated
1-1/4 cups sugar
3/4 cup all-purpose flour
1/4 cup fine dry bread crumbs

1/4 teaspoon salt
2 ounces (2 squares)
semisweet chocolate, grated
1-1/2 teaspoons vanilla extract
CREAM FILLING:
1/2 cup whipping cream
1/4 cup ground almonds
3 tablespoons sugar
FROSTING:
4 ounces (4 squares)
unsweetened chocolate
3 tablespoons butter
1 tablespoon brandy *or*
1 teaspoon vanilla
2 to 2-1/2 cups
confectioners' sugar
2 to 3 tablespoons milk
Chopped almonds for garnish

Beat the egg yolks until thick and lemon-colored. Gradually beat in the sugar; set aside. Combine flour, bread crumbs and salt. Add chocolate and mix thoroughly, but lightly. Add flour mixture to egg yolk mixture in 4 portions, folding until well-mixed after each addition. Set aside. With clean beaters, beat egg whites with vanilla extract until stiff, but not dry, peaks are formed. Stir 1 cup of beaten egg whites into yolk batter (makes batter less stiff for folding). Gently fold in remaining beaten egg whites. Turn into a well-greased and parchment-lined 9- or 10-in. springform pan or deep, round layer cake pan. Bake at 325° for 50-60 minutes. Remove from pan; cool completely. Split cake in half. Set aside. Make filling by whipping cream; fold in almonds and sugar. Spread filling on bottom half of cake. Replace top. Make frosting by melting chocolate and butter together in saucepan; remove from heat. Stir in brandy; add sugar and milk, mixing until frosting is of spreading consistency. (Work quickly as frosting sets up fast.) Frost sides and top of cake. Press the chopped almonds around sides of cake. Refrigerate for 4 hours or longer to let the flavors mellow. *Torte in photo was baked in 8-in. pan. **Yield:** 20 servings.

> *HOLIDAY HINTS:* Make a pretty pizza dip by spreading 1 8-oz. package of cream cheese on a plate and topping it with pizza sauce. Then add any or all of the following: chopped onions, peppers, tomatoes, green or ripe olives, shrimp. Top with mozzarella cheese. Serve with crackers or melba rounds. • Brighten platters of roast or fowl with bright-red crab apples. Combine with sprigs of parsley for a red-and-green holiday look.

INDEX